Learning to Take It

How I Grew to Accept Abuse

A Memoir by
Bobbie Becerra

Learning to Take It
How I Grew to Accept Abuse

ISBN -10: 1537543644; ISBN-13: 978-1537543642
Assigned by CreateSpace
Printed by CreateSpace

Author's Note

This work is intended to share personal experiences and perspectives related to child abuse and the development of attitudes toward domestic violence. My goal is to contribute to the discussion of domestic violence on a national level with a focus of trying to understand how children grow into lives of abuse.

This book is not intended to give advice or suggest a right or wrong way for individuals to handle abusive experiences. Names in this work have been changed to protect privacy as this is also not an effort to call attention to specific individuals, victims or abusers.

*Truth Speaks
Clearest
In Dreams*

Contents

Introduction

Domestic violence—maybe you had no choice as a child, but what about now? As an adult you have other options. Tell me, if things are so bad then why not just leave?

It surprises me at times that this question is still asked so frequently, but I, personally, have been asked a number of times and have overheard countless discussions about abuse and this question is almost always raised.

Though I actually appreciate and still look for chances to talk about my experience, every time I am asked this specific question, I have to manage my reaction so I don't get lost in my own panic or urgency to come up with an answer that will prove I didn't just ask for it or somehow wanted it to continue.

My first response is always an overwhelming sense of protection of my relationship with the brother I grew up with, then a physical sense of protecting myself and my mother, followed by specific memories of clarity in the middle of chaos and deception disguised as protection. So many memories flood my head in seconds with questions of how to describe situations or explain how much of life is spent just learning to "take it" so one is not completely destroyed either physically or in one's own sense of self. So many reactions at once, there is simply no clear explanation that I can verbalized in a reasonable response.

I am hoping that this effort will help people understand, without judgment, that the action required to leave an abusive situation involves far more than just making the choice to leave the abuser.

Part One:
An Unstable Foundation

*At the top of the stairs just outside the
front door, I am sitting next to her.
I know to listen carefully but still keep my
distance.*

*She looks just like her, but I can't tell
unless she looks at me.
But she just keeps looking straight ahead
so I do the same.*

*I try to get a little closer to her
to feel her skin and see if
she can feel me. Nothing.
So, I just wait until she speaks.*

"You know I am not really your mother."

*"I know.
What does that mean?"*

*"You will live here, eat here, sleep here –
people will think I am your mother, but
you will know I am not."*

*She didn't say anything else, just sat
there never looking at me. But things
suddenly made sense.*

So much waiting and guessing; I am glad I now know.

I am thankful that I will be able to sleep here and people won't ask me why I don't have a real mom.

I am really scared, though. I know there are a lot of things in the world that can hurt me.

I also know that I have to protect myself – protection is not included in sleeping here – but I don't really know how to do that.

I am only five. I don't know everything I'm supposed to look for, yet. I know some things, just not enough.

I will have to learn to pay better attention and watch very carefully.

Douglas

I've never understood how so many people say they wish they could be a kid again. When I think of myself as a kid, I still feel the stress of having so many problems, so many strange people around, so much distortion, I am absolutely clear that, given the opportunity, I would never go back. The first dozen or so years of my life, we moved around so much that I organize many of my memories based on where we lived. And it's not like we traveled the world or moved to bigger and better. Most of the movement was from one low-income apartment to the next and mostly in Los Angeles. Between Echo Park and downtown, I can walk to at least ten places that were home for a while.

I was such a serious kid—born old is how I was often described. I was credited or criticized, depending on the source, for being so specific in my attention to life and trying to learn so much so soon. We had an old painting in our living room for a while when we were over on Adams, at Fred's place. The painting was picked up from a yard sale or found on the street and was a portrait of a female that my mother described as either young and new to life's discoveries or very old and nearly destroyed by them, the viewer could not be certain which was accurate. She would tell people that she had to get the painting, because it was exactly like her daughter, somehow so overburdened but still just a child.

It did help me feel somehow acknowledged when I heard her say that, but at the same time, hearing it was very upsetting. If I was so clearly overburdened, wouldn't that be due to my need for more protection? A confronting but, I thought, fair question. I asked a lot of questions. Many I asked out loud, but some I kept in my head. This one I kept inside, at least for a while.

I am not completely sure that I was just born serious or if it was more because I felt someone had to pay attention, and I wasn't convinced my mom was capable. It may sound harsh, but I made my judgments based on what I saw.

I don't really remember the first time my mother showed that she wasn't able to deal with things. I also don't know when I first noticed that she and most people were almost always drunk. Whenever it started, I knew clearly that there were things I just couldn't count on my mom to take care of. Later, as I grew and tried to learn how to make decisions about shaping my life, I would ask about how things got started. At first, though, I just needed to pay attention to what was real at the time; I'd sort out the details later.

I know that some things happened when I was very young—too young to really remember details, more just sense memories. My brother, Roman, though, is fifteen months older than me and does remember some things that I don't. He remembers something about the car accident. That was the time we were at the Bon Aire Apartments, up the hill from

Glendale Blvd, and Mom was arguing with a friend. The details are debated, but what is agreed on is, of course, Mom was drinking when it happened. She and her friend had another argument and Silvia had walked out. My mom followed her, and while carrying me, Mom ran into the street after Silvia when the car hit us.

When Mom told the story, she said that it was Roman who ran out and she was trying to protect him. What I heard later was that Mom was desperate to end the argument and she had run into traffic. I can't say I remember, but knowing how my mother handled things, I can easily believe this is the more accurate version. In a way it wouldn't really matter, except that Mom's version made my brother the one who made the mistake that led to the accident, indirectly pointing the blame at him. For that reason, I wish she had told a different story: He was three, no blame should be placed there. Whatever the details, apparently I was hit in the head, and my face looked pretty torn up. I don't remember if the accident was before or after we were taken from her. I think it was before.

Roman also remembers something about when we were taken and placed into protective custody. Again, with this experience, I don't really recall what happened. I was just always aware of my fear of being split apart from my brother. He remembers some things but won't talk about them except to say it's nothing he wants me to think about. We were returned to Mom after a short while, though I don't know exactly how long.

It was sometime after these instances when I remember consciously recognizing that I couldn't always count on my mother. I think I was three or four years old when we were on Douglas, the place with the big red stairs, in a single apartment where we each had a bed in the main room.

Like many families, we would say prayers before sleep, and Mom would put us to bed with kisses and our own routine of saying good night and her covering us in bed. On this night we had gone through our routine, but things were different. She was not happy. She was almost afraid it seemed. She still covered me and went through all the motions as usual, but things did not seem right. I wanted her to be happy, and I wanted her to come and kiss me more. I decided then that I would play a game and keep asking for blankets so she would have to come and cover me and kiss me again. I thought I would get to do it a couple of times before she would start laughing and see that it was a game. My plan didn't work.

I asked several times for another blanket and was surprised that she just kept going. Yes, it was a little colder than usual, but we were indoors in L.A., it was not unbearable. I started exaggerating my speech and started uncovering myself before saying I was cold again. She didn't notice. The last time I asked for another blanket, she had started pacing and grasping her hands, and started talking – to herself or whoever was listening. Her voice was in a panic saying we were out of blankets. I quickly went from feeling playful to being afraid and worried that I was going to get both me and my brother in trouble even though he hadn't been at all involved in my little game but rather was asleep in his bed right next to mine.

I was scared and told her I was playing. I wasn't really cold but just playing a game. She didn't seem to hear me. She was moving in a way that seemed she was going between begging forgiveness and praying for mercy. I pushed the blankets off of me and got out of my bed.

I went up to her and told her I was sorry. I wouldn't play those games anymore. I was not cold. I didn't need the blankets. She could have them back. She didn't seem to respond. I looked at her face and directly called for her. "Mama, I'm sorry."

Then I saw it . . . and I heard the voice clearly and calmly speak in my own head. *"Oh, Mom isn't here anymore."* I was reminding myself that I'd seen this before, this is not new. *Sometimes Mom just goes away. She's not here now.* This meant that I could no longer talk about what was happening there in the room between us and would have to figure out how to talk to just her—the person in front of me—until my mom came back.

When my mom faded out, the person she would become always brought God along with her in some way. That night, she was calling out to God to help her find more blankets and not to punish her with such cold in the house.

I quickly changed my approach. I stopped saying I was sorry and stopped talking about the game. I listened to her ask God for mercy and to relieve the empty and cold house. I told her God was listening and gave her what she asked for. I used myself as proof. "See? I am out of bed with no blankets. I am not cold. God heard you." I was falsely excited in my tone. I was speaking as though I was trying to convince her that we had seen a larger-than-life miracle, and God, Himself, had changed things.

I stood with her, looking for her to come back at least enough to see where we were, then eventually to reconnect with the rest of what was real outside of her worry that she was somehow being punished. She finally looked at me, made eye contact. Then there was relief on her face; she began to cautiously smile. I smiled and said again that God heard her. In reality, the room was still cold. I still needed a couple of extra blankets but instead took one, kept my games and requests to myself, and just waited for that part of the night to pass before going to sleep.

I could never tell when my mom would check out, but as I saw and recognized that night, there were always some specific signs that told me – an absence in her eyes that kept her from really making contact when looking at me and, suddenly, somehow God was in the picture showing her some big vision that always included some kind of reminder of punishments and threats. When she was actually present, my mom was often amazing. She could hold moments of such clarity and give me pieces of information in such a complete and compassionate way, I felt I would be okay no matter what happened. Sadly, she checked out a lot, so I had to learn to count on things other than her moments of clarity and spent a lot of time looking for her and hoping she would not go away.

***

There was a lot to pay attention to. I tried so hard to get the rules down, always watching, always listening to people say what was supposed to happen, and trying to figure out how to balance what I was told the rules were against what was actually happening in life.

I know that this is something that everyone has to learn – how to balance all of the information and somehow translate it to something meaningful enough to actually be able to move through life a little easier. I was doing the same thing everyone else was doing, I guess. It's hard to tell, because there are some things that are taken for granted and you are simply not supposed to talk about . . . but then, if the things that you can't talk about are things that keep happening, how do you deal with them? Figuring this out has always been one of my biggest problems. It's challenging with so much conflicting information in general, but even more difficult when it comes to things that are really not to be discussed. Abuse is one of those things, especially if there is a sexual element involved.

I don't really remember when the molestation started, and I don't remember ever being surprised when it did. It seemed to have been a regular part of life. Again, something that isn't supposed to happen, but here it is, consistently present.

My memories of the Douglas apartment with the red stairs are limited. I know that there were strange things that happened there, and what I later found out was that we lived there just before we were taken away from Mom. I am not sure where we went from there, but sometime soon we moved to the apartment over the store on Glendale Boulevard, just off of Court Street.

I was withdrawn a bit when we were there. My mom had a friend in one of the apartments across the hall, which was good, because her friend was an older lady who played cards with her. That meant Mom would spend more time at home and not out finding men. My brother was at Head Start that year. I missed him when he went to school even though it was just a few hours a couple blocks away.

I didn't like how things were going. My mom was always looking for men to be role models for my brother, and I hated that they were all the same—either creepy guys who put their hands or mouths on me, or violent ones who were always about fighting—but she kept finding them anyway. I was also growing angry that she would bring these men around and then somehow wanted them to teach my brother something. *And, what was he supposed to learn? To always hit people and touch little girls?* I didn't get it and didn't have the words to tell her why I was upset about things.

My mother wasn't completely out of touch, though. She heard me in my own way try to voice my thoughts and tell her that I didn't agree with things. She knew that there were real questions I had about things that kept happening. That's when she started explaining to me that men and women are different. Men don't think the same way that women do. Women think and talk with their heads and hearts, and men think and talk with their fists, a message that would be repeated several times as I grew up.

At some level I know that it is true that men and women don't think in the same way, but the lines my mother drew when she described the difference translated to a hopeless vision for me. *That means the best I can look for is a man who will talk to me with his fists? That's what you are willing to teach my brother— your son?* Part of my questioning was about wanting clarity and to understand the world, but another part was intensely defensive. I know my brother; he is a loving person who shows affection easily. How dare anyone, including—or especially—his mother suggest he will never be able to love a woman without hitting her? I saw my mother having such low expectations as simply offensive and I didn't want Roman to know what she thought about men. Again, I didn't really know how to say these things yet, but the questions and objections were clearly coming up in my head.

I think my mother was going through a strange time when we were there. I am glad that she had the older neighbor lady to talk with. I remember listening to them talk, knowing that the discussion was too big for me but still getting some of the information I needed.

I heard that my mom talked about spending time with men who hurt her and how she didn't know what to do about not having a father for me and my brother. I also heard her talk about me and how much I knew. My mom would go between crediting me as an old, wise soul who helped her get through hard times with a capacity to receive more than anyone she knew and condemning me as an eye of God who saw and called out everything she did wrong. She was right that I would always listen to her talk about parts of life I was simply too young to have to be aware of, and I would question the way of the world we seemed to keep following, but it was about my trying to learn how I would live my life as I grew up. I was constantly thinking of what kind of life I would have after I was too big to be at home and would have to make my own living.

The neighbor lady seemed to ease my mom a little reminding her that I was just a girl trying to figure out how to grow up, like every other little girl does. It didn't help so much that the struggles that were building between me and my mom were gone, but at least we didn't have Jesus show up so often during that time when she had the lady to talk with.

We weren't above the store long. By the summer before it was my turn to get ready to go to school, we were with Fred over on Adams.

Fred's Place

Fred was a step up in many ways for us. He had a good job; he did drink but rarely got ugly. He would play cards and Monopoly with us. He even took us out to McDonald's when Mom was in the hospital for her surgery. He would take my little girl gifts and act like they were treasures. I had this mini doll with long hair on a key chain that I just loved, and gave to him so he would never have to drive alone. He took the gift and kept her with him every time he was in the car and would tell people his girl gave it to him. It felt good that Fred never showed any shame of us. I remember wishing that things would work out better with Fred. Of course, by this time I knew we would likely not be with him long, but I was still hoping that maybe things would be better than expected.

Our time with Fred brought its own complexities with so many conflicting lessons that seemed to come up almost constantly. His place was where we were when I started school and met my first little girlfriend who would come over and play out on the balcony. It's where we were when we would leave cookies and milk out for Santa and where we first got visits from the tooth fairy. It was where we were when my mom and I would have girls' day at home and paint our nails and style our hair while Fred and my brother would go outside and have guy time together. I started learning how to cook and was introduced to the traditional roles assigned to men and women in a way that gave credit to the value of both. In some ways our time there was close to normal and was nurturing.

While all these generally positive things were going on, there were still so many other things happening at the same time. It was at Fred's place where I had to pay attention and made what I still consider some of my most important decisions.

Fred had a few friends we would visit with. Most were people I didn't spend much time with. They would come by to play cards or dominoes and mostly to drink. I would try to keep somewhat of a distance but also to watch and learn from what I was seeing. I was always working so hard to figure things out.

I saw patterns that I didn't understand. I saw that every adult around us was always drinking. I saw that many of them would become violent when they drank. I also saw that with most couples there was one that was drunk and mean and other who would take the violent attacks. Most of the violence was from the man toward the woman, but some men had talked about deciding to never hit a woman so they ended up being the one hit. This was one of my main questions at that time—how is it that babies are born and become children who don't drink alcohol and don't beat people up, but then somewhere before reaching adulthood, they must become drunk and violent? What, *exactly*, happens? I told myself to pay attention and watch closely so that I could work to keep it from happening to me. This point was key—Today, I am not drunk and am not beating my kids or family. Maybe one day I will have to be like everyone else, but not today . . . and, if I HAD to be like everyone else, I would rather be hit than look at someone I love and hurt them. Decision made – "victim" is better than abuser.

***

The molestation also seemed to be more consistent at Fred's—not from Fred toward me, and not from just one guy who'd come by, but from several of the men who would visit. This was not only frightening, but again, just so confusing. Confusing because in our home we had so many open discussions about difficult topics, including child abuse. One rule was that we could ask anything and talk about anything. Mom may not have answers, but we could ask. We could have easily been the poster family of how to have the talk about hard topics, and there was no denying that that there are so many families dealing with sexual and domestic abuse. We saw public service announcements and talked about what my brother and I should do if anyone hurts us or touches us in a bad way. We were told to talk to our mother, or a doctor, or a police officer, or a teacher, or a friend if we were touched or mistreated by anyone—because child abuse is one of the most damaging crimes an adult can commit. Okay, lots of words, but things are not working that way. So now what?

The translation I came up with is that what is really being said is there are two kinds of rules that we live by. First, there are the "real rules," meaning the laws of life. If you stop breathing, you will die. Yes, that is a real rule, so don't stop breathing. Then there are the rules that we talk about but don't truly live by and aren't that serious. Things like you can't have dessert before dinner. Yes, this is a rule, but really, lots of people actually do break it, and I haven't seen anyone die specifically from breaking it. Okay, so now I know. There are real rules, and there are things we say are rules. Abusive acts fall under the second kind of rule, and I saw early and repeatedly that this one was often broken.

***

Two of Fred's most trusted friends were a couple who lived downtown. I don't know the relationship they had with Fred, but they were introduced as our "true" Godparents, Nino and Nina. I never knew their real names.

Nina was very sweet and warm to me; my mom loved her. Nino was a molester. I was still four when we first started going to see them. I mark my age by remembering that this was just before I started school. We would visit them in their small hotel apartment that had a tiny kitchen, a main room, a bedroom, and a walk in closet. The closet was just off the main room and was where they kept their pet bird.

When we visited, Nina would greet us with a big hug and lots of kisses. She would act so excited to see her little ones. We would all walk in through the little kitchen and sit in the front room. Then, Nino would always take me into the closet and tell everyone he was taking me to see the bird. We would go in, and I would start crying when he started touching me. The main room where my mother, Fred, and Nina were all visiting was just a few feet away from me, so everyone could hear me crying. Nino would laugh and sometimes rattle the bird cage to make more noise, then would just say in his broken English that I was still afraid of the bird. "Every time she is here she is afraid of the bird."

I've heard it said that the true damage from abuse is not only the act but the fact that you can't talk about it. In a very real way, I feel this is true to my experience. True because something happens with secrecy – it takes away any sense of reality or the acknowledgment that is needed to balance life's events. Here I was crying and trying to physically pull away from the man who called himself my Godfather and my family is just a few steps away, but I can't say what is going on. And he speaks for me, lying about the events. But, really, who are they going to believe, a four-year-old who stumbles for words to clearly say what is happening or a man who made a commitment to God that he would care for me as his own child? A lot about this experience still affects me, but the God thing just bothers me in a way I don't know how to describe. *Really, you're going to use the sense of trust in God against a child?* I still can't speak to that and not become enraged . . . a topic for a different discussion.

Nino was not the first man who touched me, nor was this the first time I had to decide how or if I should say something. The times I had spoken up in the past didn't seem to make a difference. I had told my mom after one of our "speak up" discussions that one of her friends had touched me. She explained to me that I was mistaken, but there is a real problem where a lot of kids get abused so it is important to talk about it. In this case, though, I misunderstood. The same thing happened when I talked to a neighbor and said that I didn't like it when Fred's friend came over, that he always made me cry when he would make me sit on his lap. Again, I was mistaken and too sensitive. It was the same problem when I talked about Albert, our downstairs neighbor who loved to hold me when I was wearing dresses but somehow always ended up with his hands in my underwear. So many misunderstandings! It's never denied that these things were happening, but I just misread the intent.

I thought about that when I considered what to do with Nino. I wasn't sure if my mom would believe me, but Nino was so consistent, I knew that it didn't matter, I would only need to show her. That would be easy. I would just tell her to come into the closet quietly the next time she heard me cry, and she would see for herself—no chance of misunderstanding.

Then I had to think about it. What if she did see? Then what? I would finally be believed and would be saved from more incidents with Nino, but I also knew that Mom can't handle things and would make a bigger problem. She would tell everyone. Her friends would start coming around to hear her cry. She would be the one everyone would feel sorry for and then even more strange people would start coming around. I would be the one who made the decision to do this and would have to deal with everyone seeing my mom destroyed. I had to consider the results of my actions, not just what I wanted to happen. That was an important practice that everyone needed to learn how to do in life. Be Godly and consider that Nino is sick. He doesn't need to be punished but understood. My actions will affect more than just me. I knew this was a big decision; I had to think it through.

So, I did my research and talked to a lot of people. I asked a lot about what happens when grown-ups do bad things. What happens to wives when husbands go to jail? How much does the family suffer when people are arrested? And maybe most important, what does a good person do when something bad happens to them? I got my answers, which seemed to bring up more questions. Especially the answer of what to do when someone takes action against you. A Godly person forgives. But, but doesn't "forgiveness" involve more than just "taking it"? I never got the answer to that question, but I worked so hard and spent so much time trying to figure things out that several days I would end up just crying for what seemed to be no reason.

Then I finally decided that if I really couldn't figure out the right thing to do, I would just go with the numbers. If there is no clear answer, then it must be the one that will hurt the fewest number of people. So if I stay quiet, I will keep getting hurt, but I am already hurt so that's done. If I speak up, I will hurt Nina, my mother, Fred, and my brother. Nino will also be hurt, but I can't count him because he is the one doing this, so it is not really me hurting him. I would be the one speaking up, though, and in doing so, there will be at least four other people hurt. Counting me, that's five. If I stay quiet, then only one suffers. Decision made—stick with one, stay quiet, and take it. Fortunately, the issue eventually resolved itself when Fred left. Once he was out of the house, our "true" Godparents also disappeared.

Fred's departure was somewhat sudden. It happened one day when my mom saw Fred and my brother "wrestling." It was one of the seemingly normal nights when I was in the kitchen with my mom making dinner and the guys were in the front room playing. Suddenly Mom was arguing with Fred and told him to immediately get his stuff and get out.

What she saw was Fred crossing a line with my brother. She acted quickly and absolutely. Fred was gone that night. I remember her telling me that it's not really good when things happen to girls, but any kind of molestation can completely destroy a boy. I was confused and felt a bit like a failure. I was not at all questioning that my brother should be protected. I was just thrown off by the suggestion that girls should be able to deal with it and be okay when I knew I wasn't.

Roy

Once Fred left, I started wondering what this meant for us. In one of her moments of clarity, I had talked with my mother about what God really was. She explained that God was different for everyone but that the true sense of God was in each person. She told me to look at myself, that I am the one to count on, no one or thing outside of myself. I asked her what would happen if I got sick in my head, and I couldn't count on me anymore. "That's when you go to God" was her answer. She said, "People go to God when there is nothing else." And for her, that's exactly what would happen. As soon as we were on our own, with no man in the house, I always felt a relief of not having to worry about him, but then there was a real need to watch out for her.

When we were alone strange things happened. Jesus seemed to always show up, and somehow that would mean Mom was completely lost. We went to a lot of different churches, all based in Christianity, but I still identify as being raised Catholic. I don't practice it and have never really believed the whole story on a literal level. I would listen and still try to extract lessons from the teachings, but ultimately, I never got past the basic premise of God being all loving, but the main tool used to keep people in line is the threat of hellfire. It was especially hard for me when I would watch people around me constantly look toward God for what they wanted, even if what they wanted was for their selected individuals to be struck down. It seemed that the people I was around used the idea of God as more of a means to have proof that others were simply evil and that they themselves were good and worthy of compassion. My mother took this to the extreme.

We were still at Fred's place (after he left) when the behavior got worse. She was always a little strange when talking about God. Sometimes she was so clear and so accepting. Those times she would say that everyone needs some help and some connection; hopefully they find God wherever they are. Then when she was in a different space, her talk of God seemed desperate and frightening. She would bring out the Bible a lot and would seem to find every passage that related to some example of punishment and deceitful beasts trying to trick you.

She would start reading and interpreting. Then she would have me and my brother kneel and pray for forgiveness. We would stay up till the early morning hours, listening and following instructions to pray and ask for mercy. This was such a strange part of our lives, I don't even really know how to describe it. It was scary to hear those awful stories of how the beast would destroy you and how he is everywhere trying to trick you. But the really frightening part was that I remember looking at my mom, trying to find her, and somehow she just wasn't there. I learned the only way to talk with her in those stages was to speak her language.

She would say that God talked to her and said things to her. I tried so hard to understand and make some decision about if any part of this could be true. *It's my mom, it's God, it's the Bible, so it should be true, right?*

I remember speaking to God in my thoughts. Asking Him that if all this was true, why didn't he help us figure out what to do? As the hours passed, my mental dialogue with God got more trying. *Is she still talking to you? Can you tell her we need to go to bed? At least tell her to let us stand up—my legs are tired.*

With practice, I started to learn how to shorten the sessions. My brother and I made this deal: He would pretend to be so tired that he had to go to bed and would fall asleep immediately. Then, when Mom came into the bedroom and said that Jesus had talked to her, my brother would pretend to sleep, and I would tell Mom that Jesus had also talked to me and said that my brother needed to rest so we should wait and do this tomorrow night. It would sometimes work, and if we could get through that night, we could usually get past a few more. When it didn't work completely, I would get out of bed and talk to Mom and Jesus for a while. My brother would sometimes try to break up the session by "waking up" so then we would have to stop.

Eventually things would settle down and we would not have so many Godly discussions. When that happened, the drinking got worse. It was always scary when she drank so much, but it also made me more and more angry. I didn't feel sorry for my mother when she was drunk. I felt abandoned, especially since she knew things got bad when she was drinking so much but it happened over and over again. Then Mom would be back to looking for a dad for us.

One night, after one of her dates, things went bad, and there was someone there fighting Mom. My brother and I hid in the bedroom until it was quiet. Then I went out to see how things were. My mom was crying and the guy was gone. I had seen Mom cry before, but this time was so much worse. I felt like what I saw was more than fearful tears; I felt like this was the first time I saw her really broken. Yes, there were many things that I was angry about and I knew she couldn't handle everything, but she was still my mom. And a part of me still thought that she was stronger than anyone else. This time, I started seeing that I had to give up that thought even if I didn't want to. I knew she needed something to lift her up, but I didn't know how. I wanted to understand and figure out some way to get us past all of this, but where do I start? I decided to be direct.

"Why do we keep living like this?" Living like this meaning we are okay and safe for a while, then someone comes and hits her or is hurtful to us, then God shows up, then she's always drunk, and then we start again. We kept losing the space of a safe home, and we always ended up having to watch out and be careful who gets upset. *Why?*

I had no words to speak my thoughts in whole, but Mom did realize my question was valid, not one she could just distract from. She also felt the depth of the topic and the reality that she didn't know how to explain it. She quickly worked to clear her head and change her expression. She looked up at me and answered, "That's just the way it is. Now, let's clean up."

That's it? Just the way it is? So life is a series of getting hit and having your home destroyed by an angry man, and then you have to clean up and wait for the next round? No. Not for me. I love you, Mom, but here is where I won't follow. I will not let myself have a life like this. Not today, not when I grow up.

My thoughts were so clear and so full of anger toward my mom, who was actually telling me that I would need to get used to this. I tried to look at her with some compassion but just wanted to cry that this was the reality of my life at five. *This is too much to handle, I don't want to be here.*

"Okay." I went along and started picking things up while my mom got a broom. I told her Roman was sleeping so she wouldn't call him out to join us. It worked. Roman stayed in the room, and I did what I could to get my mom to be okay. I started picking up some of the larger things that had been knocked off shelves but weren't broken. She started to sweep up the smaller broken things so I didn't have to risk getting cut. Going through the motions to improve our home together helped her, but I kept my mental position and made a commitment that this is where I would not follow my mother's ways. I would *never* live like this . . . one of many promises I made to myself and failed to keep.

***

As we went along, I would continue to look around and question why people did things. I would look for examples of lives that I wanted to have when I grew up. I found lots of examples of what I didn't want but none of what I wanted. People would ask me what I wanted to be when I grew up, and I couldn't think of anything other than what I didn't want. I knew I didn't want to be drunk, I didn't want to get hit, I didn't want to scare my kids. I really couldn't imagine what kind of life I would have, so I started to try to imagine something.

I would spend time thinking of what I wanted if I were to make it to adulthood. I would first and foremost be trustworthy. I would be known as someone who would offer comfort and help people figure out ways to make life easier. I wasn't sure if I would have kids. I didn't want kids if they would have to see my husband hit me, so if I had kids I would have to first find a man who loved me and would not hurt me.

When I would talk to my mom, she would be very supportive and encouraging about my being a person who could listen to anyone about anything, but she helped me understand I was unlikely to find a man who would *never* hit me. Again, she would tell me about how men talk with their fists, that men can't handle things so they get overwhelmed and rule physically.

This explanation would come up regularly when I would talk about my life as an adult. Mom would keep telling me that I may find a man who liked me, but I would need to know how to be a woman who didn't make her man hit her.

What Mom told me didn't really scare me about my life at that time. On some level I thought she was wrong: There is no way I will believe that ALL men hurt women. I don't have any proof of that yet, except for the few men who chose to get hit instead. But I also didn't want to be like that. More important, though, in case anyone has forgotten—I have a brother. There is no way I am willing to put him in the category of men who can't think with their heads. This is the part of the message that just infuriated me.

"You have a son! Did you forget?" is what I wanted to scream out to her. Instead I responded to her blanket statement about violent men with a question. "Even Roman?" She told me that Roman was special and that he would be one of the very few men who could think and wouldn't have to hit his wife.

Aha! So it's not ALL men, right?

Yes, Mom conceded that it was true. Not ALL men hurt women. I would, however, need to understand that those men are few and far between. I would also need to understand that I would be very lucky to find any man who would be willing to marry me, let alone one who would not hit me.

This was another theme that was regularly repeated. I would have to accept that my husband, if I got one, would certainly hit me. *Okay, but why?* I would challenge her on this, because I just didn't get why I would be the one woman who simply had NO chance of having a husband who loved me and didn't hit me.

It was a very good thing that we were allowed to ask questions simply because it gave me permission to think that what I am told may not be what is real, so I would ask a lot of stuff and often would listen and put away the answers I got for another day so I could find something to disprove what I had been told. My mom had told me several times that because I was never going to be like normal women I would have a hard time finding a husband, I was too fat and too ugly. But the thing she really stuck with was that the real problem was I was too smart. If I wanted to keep from getting hit, I would have to learn to play dumb, and she knew I wouldn't do it.

What!? I'm too smart, so that means I can't be loved and cared for? Now that just doesn't make sense.

I was very clumsy in my word selection, but I did tell her I thought she was mistaken. "If I am a smart girl like you keep saying I am, then won't I grow to be a smart woman? Doesn't that mean maybe a smart man will like me?"

"No." I was corrected and again she tried to explain that it is okay to know some things, but the worst thing a woman can be is smart. When I think of one specific conversation I had with her, I wish I could show a video without the sound. Anyone watching would see this loving mother sitting with her daughter at eye level, stroking her little girl's hair, leaning in with her face nearly touching the girl's, and saying something so gently. But then turn up the volume and listen to what is said. She was telling me that no matter what, even if no man would love me, she always would. And somehow we would find a husband, even if we had to *trick* him to like me, we would find him . . . and when he hits me it will be okay, because she would always love me.

I remember that conversation and being so confused at having this soft touch and gentle voice comforting me but still telling me I am not deserving of love other than hers or that of someone who will hurt me. It was effective enough to suggest that maybe she was right, and if she was, I didn't really know what I could do.

***

Weeks passed; I was tired and at a point where I couldn't imagine how I could keep going and not break. I was starting to believe things my mother said about me and didn't see anything that would make me think that things would change with so many strange men around, with Mom going into her cycles, with any of it. I wasn't just quitting, I was acknowledging defeat. I had already spent too much time being afraid. I looked around and tried to deal with the things that kept happening. I tried to talk to people to tell them I had real problems I needed help with. The message that kept coming back was, "There is no way a five-year-old can know what a real problem is. It only gets harder as you grow up." Oh God! If this is true—and it seems to be since so many adults have told me this—then there is no way I am going to make it. I can barely hold myself together now. I am so angry and so much at a loss for possibilities. I think I just have to make the decision and figure out the details.

What about God? Well, God, if you really made me and love me then you have to help me or forgive that I will never be okay. My heart is black. That's the heart you made in me. It is poisoned, and there is no cure. If this was not true, then these things would not keep happening, and I would not have to prepare for a life with no one loving me unless I trick them. I ask for help and I am told it is just me, so maybe it is. Forgive me or don't . . . the only thing I ask is that my brother is okay.

After speaking to God in my thoughts, I went on to plan my method. Mom had been very direct about a lot of things in the house. Hands off of the chemicals under the sink and any medication: The chemicals are never supposed to be eaten, and medication can only be taken when you are really sick. Either will kill you if misused. With this information, I knew the two options I would consider: bleach or pills.

The bleach was my first choice just because there was always a big bottle that is easy to get to. I could always be in the kitchen by myself for several minutes, and if I did it while she was napping I would have a whole hour. Yes, bleach was a good first choice. The only problem I saw, once I thought it through, was that I didn't know what would actually happen or when. Would I drink down a bottle and die there in the kitchen? That would be bad if my brother were to find me. I don't want anyone to be hurt, especially not him. I won't run that risk, so I will stick with pills; pills always take a little time.

Most medicine was kept in the bathroom cabinet, but there were two Mom kept in the drawer near her bed. She monitored those, so clearly they were the strongest ones and the best to choose for the job. The nitros were too risky; she actually counted them at night to be sure we didn't take any. The other one that she took when she was hurting and couldn't sleep was the one to try. I didn't know what it was, but I snuck into her drawer and took some before going to bed. I kissed her and my brother good night and reminded God that I am the one who couldn't get it right, not my brother—he needs to be protected. Then I laid down and was ready to just not wake up.

Well, clearly I hadn't taken enough or just made the wrong choice. I did not have a peaceful sleep into a world of final relief but instead woke up with terrible pain and disorientation. I was vomiting blood and couldn't walk straight. I know it scared my mom, because I was violently sick and never gave a clue about the reason. She stayed up with me while I was sick and cleaned me up once I was finally finished heaving. I eventually went back to bed and slept several hours.

When I got up later I was still a little disoriented, but it was clear that my attempt had fallen short. I was not relieved or at all apologetic that I had made the attempt and failed. I was angry . . . angry with my mom, angry with my life, angry with God. I had no words to speak out loud but plenty to say in my angry mental confrontation with God.

I've asked you over and over for help. I've looked at myself so I don't blame everyone else. I've tried to understand and ask people to help me. Nothing has worked. And now, even when I tell you I can't make it, my heart is too weak, you refuse to allow me to rest?!

How can you say that you are a loving God and want me to believe things will get better . . . that all I need to do is try and stay forgiving? No! It's not getting better. I don't believe you! Prove it.

Either show me there is something better, or I will do it again and I will do it better. I will learn and won't make a mistake again. Want me to stay here? Prove it. Quickly!

Believers would say that God was listening.

I went on day by day, trying to manage my anger when I looked at my mom's face. Trying to be there just because my brother didn't deserve to find his sister dead, trying to figure out how to keep my head up and hold any sense of hope that life is good. Then, finally, Roy showed up.

***

I have had two experiences in my life where I met someone and I swear I *felt* them before I saw them. The first time was with Roy.

We were still living in Fred's place, but without Fred there to help pay for things, we needed to leave very soon. My mom had been diagnosed with a degenerative bone disease and had filed for disability, but at the moment we were living on welfare—just as we had for as long as I knew. She was looking for ways to make some money and had a friend who knew an old blind man who needed some general housekeeping and errands taken care of, so we got on the bus and headed over to Alvarado to meet him. The first time we were there, we knocked but got no answer, so we went back a second time.

His home was on a hill near the freeway. As we walked up the long flight of stairs for the second time, I kept my head down and tried not to talk. I was angry almost every moment, so speaking would not be helpful. I just wanted to get through this and hoped that we would get home quickly.

This time when we got there, I knew he was there, because I heard his dog barking. Last time there was no dog. My mom knocked on the door, and we waited for him to answer. Just a moment before the door opened, I suddenly felt a deep change in me. The anger had subsided and I felt mixed between overwhelming excitement and complete relieving comfort. Then, when he came to the door, all I wanted to do was throw my arms around him and tell him I loved him. I remember having such a strong urge to reach out to him and then having an immediate thought that reminded me it would not be seen as normal. I told myself I was a kid, so I would just pretend I didn't know what I was doing, it was too important not to tell him how much he relieved me. I did, however, choose to keep my feelings to myself and simply said hello when I was introduced. I wasn't sure what was going to happen, but I was very happy when he welcomed my mother and invited us in.

***

I knew our time with him would be short, but I still credit Roy's being in my life as a gift that helped save me. We ended up moving in with him shortly after the first meeting and were with him less than a year.

In that time, however, we were in a place I had wished for but had not yet seen. Mom was sober and, I am tempted to say, even happy. There was no presence of violence or sexual abuse. We all enjoyed each other like a family with a sense of trust I had not known in the past. Things were good, very good.

I was still very dark in a lot of ways and regularly became very tired and depressed. My mom had no idea how to deal with me, so she would talk with Roy and he would reach out to me. Roy was older and had learned a lot about life. He was not born blind but lost his sight in an accident as an adult and went through a hard time with having to face his own way of dealing with things. I didn't know any of this at the time, but he was at a place where he could help my mom with me and could help to acknowledge me simply by showing up and hearing me say that I was lost.

I knew he was leaving the night he died. It was sometime around the holidays, but I don't remember exactly when. He would sometimes have chest pains and would walk to the back door for air. Usually it was okay, but this night was different. I walked into the kitchen and saw my mom walking him to the back door and knew this was good-bye.

My mom had told me and Roman to go and pray. We did as we were told and went into the bedroom and got on our knees. I still remember, though, how my prayer was not one asking God to spare his life and not take him. I knew he wasn't mine to keep. My prayer was one of gratitude. I wanted God to tell Roy how much I loved him and that I knew how much he had given me, to tell him it's time to rest and that he would always be loved.

I thought of a dozen moments when Roy showed me the beauty of the world around us, taught me how to dial a phone with my eyes closed, reminded me to appreciate all the small parts that made the whole, stood next to my mom with excitement and asked her to describe my face when I discovered the gift he had bought me on my sixth birthday. He loved me and showed it every day. I could spend hours talking about my time with Roy and still often escape into my memories when I need to be reminded of what comfort can look like, but like that night, for now I will just give thanks that he was with me for a while. We left Roy's place and headed to Barstow early the next year.

Part Two:
Trade-Offs

It's hot.
There is nothing out here but dirt.

I know I should just try to run, but
I have to try to make my mom leave with me.

He's already there with her,
already in his holy robe.
She is dressing in hers and telling me to get ready.

He looks at me, smiling,
knowing he has already won.
I try to get my mother to look at me
but she never faces me.

I tell her anyway.
He's not of God; he is lying.
We can't go with him; he's going to kill us.

She still doesn't listen,
but keeps dressing.

He is going to kill us. Can't you see that?
He is going to make you do it and you're just
going to say yes.

She finally turns to me,
puts her hands on my shoulders.

"He's just going to make things easier –
It's important to just do what he says.

Now, close your eyes"

Barstow

Mom found us a place in Barstow. A duplex with a full one-bedroom unit on each side, but the wall between the bedrooms had been opened up so it was now one big place. The front side opened to a room we used as the regular front room where the grown-ups would visit. To the left was the kitchen and bathroom and to the right was a bedroom where Roman and I had twin beds and two nightstands between us.

You could walk through our room to the adjoining bedroom that was part of the back unit; that was Mom's room. Then, you could walk through to the back room with its separate entrance and on to what would have been a second kitchen. Both of those rooms were designated as space for the kids to play and for the dogs when it was too cold outside. Buster and Poncho had made the move with us from L.A. and guarded the back entrance to the kid's space. But they weren't with us for long. Poncho was old and getting very sick when Mom had him put down. Buster was still young and strong, but he was put down at the same time. I guess Mom thought she had too many lives to take care of when she did it. I don't really know what happened, but that was a decision I know my brother had not forgiven her for.

When we first moved in, we had just enough money to get us through the first month. Then, we needed the SSI check to cover rent and food. I've always guessed that there was a detail my mom had missed so paperwork just wasn't processed on time. Whatever the reason, there was a delay, and the check didn't come when we needed it. We were out of money and soon would be out of food. Disappointing, but not the first time we were in need.

Of course, it's not like there was no help around us. Roman and I did go to school where we got tickets with the date printed on them that we could use to get lunch. We also had made friends with the family who lived in the house in back, on the other side of the yard. They shared dinners with us a few nights when my mom was out.

Luckily, not having any money didn't stop my mother from going to the bar next door most nights, as there are always ways to get drinks and cigarettes provided at no cost. We did get to a point, though, where we really needed some more help; some friendly neighbors and the random guy she got to pick up her tab weren't going to be enough.

So, doing what she knew would work, my mother got ready early one day, made a point to go sober and get cleaned up, and then walked over to the bar next door and asked for a job. When she was told no job was available, she asked for food. She didn't get a handout right away but instead got an offering to provide something if the money didn't come in a few days. That was a success. She would take the offering and would come back to ask for food again if she had to.

A few days later, when we were down to empty shelves in the kitchen, she went back. I think the owner was trying to avoid falling for the pleas of the local beggar woman and her kids, but he did take some pity on her and must have asked something about us because she came back to the duplex and told me and Roman to come on with her and say hello to the bar owner.

I remember walking into the bar as nervous as I always was when I would have to go and see if my mom was going to cause some kind of trouble. I had already learned how to talk to the police and ask people to break up fights, but I still didn't have the stomach for it and was always on alert to note the exits and be ready to run.

It was daylight and the place was empty other than the bar owner and us. That was a relief. I could usually talk to a sober man who was clear about what he wanted to say—I just still wasn't good at talking to the drunk ones. The man's face seemed to fill with some kind of recognition when I looked at him. I was worried that there would be challenges and arguments that I would have to deal with, again explaining to someone that my mom just had a lot to worry about and that we weren't wanting to start any fights, but he seemed actually kind in his expression, not at all mean. I imagined he saw that no matter what his opinion of my mom was, there really were two kids in her care, and he didn't have any desire to see kids worry about if they would have food in the house.

We were there only a moment before the man offered us sandwiches—pigs' feet sandwiches, to be exact. We got to take a couple with us and went back home while my mother stayed at the bar. We accepted his gift and gratefully shared the sandwiches for the next two days. Then the check finally came.

***

Barstow was a strange place for us. I was so nervous and always looking for signs of where we were going next, how we were going to live. We had already been plenty of places where scary things came with us and bad things kept happening. Then, we had a time when things felt good for a while. We had just left Roy's place in L.A.—a place where, for nearly a year, things were better, brighter. We had been with someone who loved us, and the anger seemed to be calmed. Now that time has passed and we're at a crossroads. I don't want to go back to a life where all the anger and fear was, but I am not at all certain that we won't.

I would look at my mom and wonder if she knew there was a way to live without all the screaming or if our time of peace with Roy was a surprise for her. I thought of my fight with God when I demanded proof that things could be better—they had to be—and then proof showed up.

So it's not impossible for us to live better again. We know now. We've been shown there's a better way. We don't have to go back. Right?

My mom seemed to also hope that we could stay in a better place. She wanted to move into our new home without the demons following us, so she found someone to come and bless each room as she had done with some other places. She was so serious about it, but with her absent energy, not her confident one. I wanted to believe that going through this ritual of having someone sprinkle holy water and praying in each room would help, but I was not convinced.

I would test things and look for signs, but as it happened in the past, there were so many conflicting things. Mom had gone back to lots of drinking and spending time with scary people. She would go into her spells sometimes where she seemed to lose any sense of seeing me, and she would suddenly start hearing things from Jesus and praying to God. The praying was always a bad sign. And I would constantly watch her temperament. It was never good when she would get angry or panic and go to God for answers when things went wrong, like when she dropped a dish, or if a light burned out, or if she lost something. It was good when she would see that things happen for whatever reason and that nobody had to be hurt because of it. That was one of the ways I could tell if she was in a clear head, how she responded when everyday things would happen. I just had to watch and see what mind she was in, so I could manage my actions around her.

I was trying not to stay so angry with her and decided to just "grow up" and start doing more to help make our home what was needed. I think Mom was trying too.

I remember one day we had the water shut off for some reason, and she had told me and my brother to go and make sure that all the faucets were turned off before we all left the house. We knew the water would be turned back on sometime while we were gone, and we had to be sure we wouldn't come home to wet floors. So we went and did what she asked, making sure all the faucets were turned off tight. Then we all left for the day to run errands and get groceries.

We were gone several hours and returned early that evening. There were no bus stops nearby and we had a lot of things to carry, so we came back by taxi which had stopped just past the front door. We got our bags and started walking to the house. Then I saw it. Water was seeping out from under the front door and down the front step. *Oh . . . now what?*

I was immediately scared and had racing thoughts to sort through. *Tell her it was me, not Roman . . . Tell her not to get mad . . . Tell her you're sorry and that you'll fix it . . . Tell her we don't have to pray or ask God who did this . . . Tell her something before it gets bad.*

I didn't know what to say or do, so I just watched my mom to see what I needed to manage. After a moment of looking, to my surprise, she didn't seem bothered at all. She just said, "Okay, let's run in and turn the faucets off." No anger, no questions, no punishment. I took that as my final sign that things were going to be better. After seeing that my mother was able to go into the house that was a wet mess in three rooms and not get mad or ask God for pity, or do anything other than just clean up, I told myself that I would have to start to relax and trust that we are moving in the right direction. Mom is really trying, or maybe she doesn't have to try but has really seen that we can be happier and she is ready to be. I have to stop testing so much. I have to trust that we will be able to be happy, not always scared.

So I did. I stopped testing, but I did keep looking for reassurances that I was accurate in my assessment. Happily, I found what I was looking for. Even if she spent time with some of the strange people, she didn't bring a lot of them to the house. She enjoyed cooking, we listened to music, she talked to us about saving money, and we even saved enough to buy a swing set that she put up for us in the backyard. We certainly hadn't achieved a feeling of being at ease, but all of these things were good signs. So I started to relax.

Then came the day when there was a knock at the door. I was in the bedroom, and my mom was in the kitchen. We weren't expecting anyone so I immediately stood at attention and watched my mom walk over to the door. The second she opened it, I swear, before I even saw him, I felt every bit of his energy flood the house; I was full of terror instantly. I wasn't sure what was at the door, but I knew it needed to stay out. I wanted to force my mother away when she started to pull the door open, or at least grab my brother and make a run for it. Not possible. I stood still, just watching and hoping that my mother would keep the unwanted outside.

My fear grew stronger when I heard his voice greet her and heard my mom's voice speak in a relieved and rescued tone when she said his name. My heart then sank when I watched my mom embrace him and invite him in. I knew then this wasn't a short visit or a pleasant reunion. This was a change in direction. No more testing or hoping or searching for a better way. It was clear at that moment that the decision was made; we were going the wrong way, back to where we were before.

Learning to Take It

Leonard

I didn't like Leonard. Or, to be more accurate, I knew I couldn't trust him. I could see with no distraction this man was harmful and untrue. I knew I would have to make it clear up front that even if he could fool my mom, my eyes were open and I could see what he was.

When we were introduced to him, my brother did what he was taught and shook his hand and called him "sir." Leonard, of course, acted as though he was a true friend and asked Roman to call him by his first name. Roman liked the permission and dropped the "sir" quickly. While I am watching this, I want to scream at my mother and tell her that she is wrong in letting this man talk to Roman . . . *Roman is trusting and he will do what this man says—that can't happen. Don't you know that?*

My turn. I knew I had no chance of getting away, and even if I somehow could, Roman would still be with him. So, I tried to do whatever I could to let this man know I would not fall for his "buddy" routine. I made sure to keep my head up and face him eye to eye. I answered questions as appropriate but made no effort to offer any warmth or sense of invitation. I kept my body tense and ready to put up a fight that moment if he attempted to touch me. I stood my ground, looking only at Leonard until the introduction was finished. I refused to give my mother even a glance after she had brought this man to meet me. I relaxed only when the two left to go to the bar. I knew this one was going to be worse than the others. This one was smart, he had my mom wrapped around his finger, and he was going to try to break me.

***

Of course, in just a short while, Leonard had started staying with us. He took the role of the replacement father but played the angle of being a friend who just wanted to have fun. I hated him and couldn't stand any time he even casually touched me. He knew how I felt and liked to play games with me. He would tell me quietly that he would get me to do what he wanted. Simple things that he would want me to do, he would tell my mom to have me do them, and then he would come and whisper to me that he always knew how to get me to do things.

Leonard was more than just another creepy guy; he was dangerous. Dangerous meaning that somehow I knew that he would not be amused with simple fondling or embarrassing me. He would hurt me— physically maybe—but more important, he would take away my hope and maybe make my brother stop loving me.

I knew I wouldn't be able to keep myself safe long, but I hoped that our time with him would fade quickly as it had with some of the others. That hope died one day when my mom was in another one of her panicked Jesus prayers and was frantically going through her drawers and asking Jesus to help her. I was impatient with her and sharply told her to stop because Jesus wasn't going to look through the drawers for her. I asked her what she was looking for and told her that she would have to find it herself. I sarcastically showed her how to open the drawers and look for something without crying by physically going to a drawer, pulling it out, and exaggerating my facial expression as though I was looking closely at what was there. She calmed down and said she was looking for a very important paper. It was one of the most important things that she would ever need to do. I told her I would help and looked for the folded paper that she described. A few minutes later she rejoiced in finally finding it. I was relieved that this little trial was over and asked her what was so important. It was her divorce paper! Now she could show that her marriage to my father was legally over, so she and Leonard could get married. I felt stupid for trying to help her find it. Now we're stuck.

***

It was a small wedding with just me, Roman, and a couple of witnesses. We soon left the duplex and moved to a place with one of Leonard's friends. It was here where things happened that were darker than I could have imagined. This is where I made what I considered a truly unforgivable mistake; I broke.

We were at the home of what I think was an old friend or maybe some old relative of Leonard's for a short while. The old man living there was almost completely bedridden with very limited movement. He would sometimes crawl naked from his room to the bathroom in the middle of the night. Mom would tell us to remember we were in his home, and he was very sick. But still, the sight was pretty scary for young kids, especially when the man is really a stranger.

We stayed there for a couple months, I think. Most of what I remember was being afraid and closely watching Leonard. He still enjoyed reminding me that he had control and would show me in little ways like asking my mom a question and then suggesting a different position after she responded. He knew how to make sure she would always agree with him.

He did this to make me do things, meaningless things. If he asked me if I wanted more to drink and I said no, he would go and say something to my mom and then my mom would demand that I have more to drink. Leonard would then just look and smile at me. His little games were about letting me know he was in control. Since he could steer my mom in any direction he wanted, that meant he was in complete control of me.

I would ask my mom when we were alone why she would always change her mind for him or why she wouldn't listen to my answer but only his. She would very quietly tell me to go along, and that Leonard was the man of the house now. I wasn't quite sure if she just believed that we were supposed to do what he said because that is the role of the woman or if she was actually afraid of him. I took the position that it couldn't be fear. She already knew him, had welcomed him, and married him. How could she be afraid and still welcome him with such relief?

Whatever the reason, I knew that Mom would always take his side, so again I was reminded that I would not be able to count on her. I tried to tell myself that when it really mattered, it would be different, so I kept trying to give her credit and to look to her as a mother who was really doing her best to take care of me.

Up to this point, Leonard's actions felt very threatening, but his actual sexual advances were not the same as what I was around before; they were much less directly physical, so it seemed that I had nothing to complain about. Somehow, though, he was terrifying compared to the others. The other guys were stupid and irritating. They were always into sneaking in disgusting touches. They scared me and hurt me, but they were not smart enough to really be cruel . . . Leonard was cruel.

Leonard didn't touch me, rub against me, or display himself to me in the beginning. What he did was *invite* me. It started at the duplex when he would sleep with my mom. After sex, he would call me into the room when Mom went to the bathroom and would ask if I wanted to know how my mom made him feel good. Then he'd laugh and say he would show me one day. The invitations continued at the new place. It would happen in the middle of the day or in the early evening when he was just lying around in his underwear, and my mom was busy doing other things. He would call me over and ask if I wanted to see him, moving his hand down his stomach to his crotch. It was disgusting. He scared me, but beyond fear, I was angry. How was it possible that this man, my mother's husband, was doing this? I wanted to cry but was determined to stay strong and take whatever kind of embarrassment or threat he was trying to inflict.

Don't cry, don't look down, don't follow his hand, don't look away—stand up and face him.

I reminded myself in my mental dialogue that if I break now, I would not have anywhere to go, so I would always just look at him very strongly, directly at his face with bold eye contact, and refuse his offer. He would then ask if I wanted to touch him or if I wanted him to see me with my clothes off. I would always stay standing, never allowing my body to weaken or my head to bow down, and would just keep saying no. He would eventually start laughing and would tell me one day I would say yes—one day I would be the one asking him to touch me.

I would never respond to those comments and would just ask if that was it and if I could go. "Yes." I would finally get permission after going through the invitation ritual.

We would go through this horrible ceremony frequently enough for me to know when to expect it. It got to where I would just interrupt the dialogue and tell him, "I still don't want to see you," in the hope that we would get through it quickly. He would try different things like offering to let me choose where we would go the next time we went out as a family or would agree that he wouldn't make my mom change her mind at dinner next time. I never knew what to say or think about these proposals. Still, more angry and offended is what I felt. I remembered that adults always think kids are so stupid, but he had to know I wasn't. This had to be part of the game he enjoyed playing, knowing that it didn't matter if I got to make some decision about our next outing, because he would still be the one in control of my mother's moves. So I would just stick with my regular reaction, trying to look strong and saying no without showing that he was bothering me. I stayed pretty strong until he tried a new move with a comment one day. "I bet Roman would say yes."

Don't cry, don't cry, don't cry . . . That was the first rule. Then I just needed to answer.

"Roman doesn't come in here." That was my way of saying that this mess was between us; Roman isn't involved.

"But I can call him." His tone was not his usual casual invitation or mocking condescension; this tone was a threat, pulling rank and reminding me that he would bring anyone into this game that he wanted.

I stayed quiet for a minute and then asked if I could leave. He knew he had gotten to me, so he enjoyed his victory and let me go. I knew I'd have to keep a close eye on Roman, so I could intervene if he was called in. But for now, Leonard was finished playing.

***

I don't remember how much time went by, but his threat to call in my brother was soon followed by a very scary and painful night. The night of my unforgivable mistake was the last time I looked to my mom to help me with Leonard, and it was the first night I felt a deep sense of almost-crippling defeat.

It was the '70s and the "all bodies are beautiful" idea was going around. So, sticking with the important lesson of being free with our bodies, Leonard told me and Roman to go on and take off our clothes. It was not a sexual setting. We were all at home, the old man was in his room, Leonard and Mom were at the table, and Roman and I were in the front room.

Roman thought it was fun and went along, but I said no. I wanted to keep my clothes on. I said that if it was about being free, then I should not be forced to undress. I asked my mom if I had to take my clothes off, and at first she agreed and said no, I could keep them on.

Leonard went on for a few minutes about personal freedom and how it was all my choice. Then he spoke quietly to my mom, and she suddenly changed her position. She told me to take my clothes off, because she was my mother and I needed to do what she said. Leonard played his angle and came to my defense, saying it was my choice, but Mom stuck with her right to tell me what to do and my job was to do it. I asked if we could just go to bed. Roman could, but I would not be excused until I did what I was told.

So after a failed attempt at a standoff, I cried quietly, took off my clothes, and sat there with my feet up on the couch and my arms around my knees, trying to hold any sense of personal modesty I could while not making any crying sounds. Leonard gave me a smile and stayed at the table with my mom.

I sat there for a few minutes to try to toughen up and stop crying long enough to find my voice and again ask permission to go to bed. I was not smooth or respectful in my request. I was rude in my tone and directed my question to my mother. "Now that I've done what you told me to do and I took my clothes off, can I go to bed?" Permission was denied. My mother strongly matched my tone and said no. A few minutes later, I heard Leonard tell her that I didn't need to stay there; it was time to let me go to bed. Then I was permitted to go.

I knew that night that I was not strong enough to stay tough and keep up with his games. I knew he was stronger, smarter, and older than me, and he had made it clear that he would use anything to break me. He had already mentioned Roman, and that night had showed me Leonard would have no problem dragging him into this awful game by having him undress. I knew looking to my mom for help was a waste of time, so I would have to change my strategy, which I did. The next time he called me into the bedroom when he was alone, he reminded me that he had helped me with my mom by letting me go to bed that night. I knew there was nothing I could say, and no one would help me, so it was now about trying to make things as easy as possible and making an attempt to keep Roman out of it. So this time I did not stand strong and look into his eyes, but instead I bowed my head, called him sir, and went closer as he had always wanted me to . . . a decision I understand but still have not truly forgiven myself for, as it did not help keep things manageable or offer any sense of protection for anyone, but just gave him a win, and then we moved on to the next round.

I still hate Leonard.

***

Mom seemed to be getting a little more stressed. She started asking things like where I had been and if I was with Leonard. I think something must have happened between them. There was this time Leonard told me and my brother to get in the car and go with him. He wasn't threatening but was moving fast and playfully like he had a fun idea. We followed, and he took us out for ice cream. No threats, no games— just a fun outing.

While we were out, Leonard told us he hadn't told Mom that we were gone so we stopped at a pay phone and he called her to tell her that he took us. He was strange in his tone with her, like he was keeping a secret. Later when we got home, I saw my mom was really scared and angry. She was washing dishes, and her hands were shaking. We then made a secret agreement that no matter what, we wouldn't say no to Leonard, but we would find a way to let her know where we were going, even if we just went in the house like we were playing and told her we were pretending to run away. I recognized her fear as she tried to sound lighthearted. He was doing the same thing to her as he was doing to me—letting her know that if he wanted to, he could do things to hurt and control her without ever touching her. Leonard didn't try to secretly take us again. I think he made his point.

After a short while it was time to move on to the next place. I think the old man told Leonard it was time to go, and it was just a short while after that we moved on. We ended up in the projects, a low-income housing community somewhere still in Barstow. The units were mostly single-story family duplexes with some single units. We had our own front lawn and shared a community area in back.

Like most of our homes, we only stayed in the Barstow projects a few months, but so many things happened there. When we first got there, Leonard was with us. I was trying to look at things with some hope that we had come to some kind of agreement that if I didn't put up much of a fight, we would just go through what he wanted, and the rest of life would be easier.

In some ways the agreement seemed to be followed. I would not fight when he told me to undress or told me he wanted to touch me, and he would let me leave the table or go outside and play without any argument or mind games. And, I had learned to deal with what he wanted. There was no hitting or penetration, but a lot of touching and watching. I learned to play the go-along to get-along game and kept waiting for things to change. *Yes, I know they got married, but he can't stay forever. They never do.*

There was other stuff going on, though. Something was changing. I tried to stay out of things as much as I could. I would do what I had to do with school and housework but didn't go out of my way to do anything more. I couldn't stand being with my mom while Leonard was in the house. Why bother? She had already shown that his word was the one she would follow even though she didn't trust him. I grew more angry with her but tried to keep thinking that she was just too blind to see what was in front of her. *Mom doesn't know what's going on, and I'll keep it that way.*

So I didn't talk to her much outside of what normal things were happening that day. I would get tired a lot and sometimes slept during the day. If I said I was tired, I was always allowed to nap—as long as I was nude. That was how Leonard wanted it. He would sometimes stand in the doorway of the bedroom and watch me, but as long as I said I was resting he would only stand quietly and look. I used that to my advantage and rested almost every day, whether I was tired or not, just so I could get a little time not thinking about if he was going to touch me. I learned to manage my time and predict his behaviors and dealt just with him—not my mom—for a lot of things.

We went along with this system for a little while. Then Leonard started saying things to his friends. We would have people over, and Leonard would wait until my mom was in the kitchen cooking or getting drinks then he'd call me over to stand next to him. He'd put his arm around me and tell the guys there that I was his. I still don't know how to describe the feeling of his touching me and presenting me the way he did. I was always full of so many feelings that there was no way to filter them. I was worried that he was going to bring someone else into this little game, and I feared that the new player would be worse than Leonard. I was worried that Roman would eventually know about all the terrible things that were happening and be forced to take part. I worried that my mom was already unaware, she wouldn't know what to do if something worse happened.

I listened to and watched everything I could to manage my place in the situation and keep things from escalating. I knew his showing me to these men was just his way of telling them that he was good at controlling me, so I played my part and stood very close to him, showing silent agreement that yes, Leonard was in control.

I watched the reactions of the men there and was somewhat shocked at their responses. No one objected, no one questioned my safety, no one suggested that maybe I was too young for this, and no one even had an objection about how he was married and his wife, my mother, was in the kitchen adjacent to the living room where we all were. I was trying to learn something here, comparing the spoken lessons of how horrible sexual abuse is to the things I was living every day. I thought about how it is especially bad on children and how it can destroy lives. But again I myself am in the middle of not just one or two situations of abuse but a whole group of people who seem unconcerned about anything being wrong here. I had to redirect my thinking. If I tried to make sense of the rules, I would break down. I had to remind myself that this is a place where the rules of protecting children simply don't apply, so I had to throw them away and pay attention to what was happening in the immediate moment.

I kept my attention on the group's reaction and listened as some guy asked Leonard if he would let me spend time with him. Leonard was clear that I was not for sharing but told some other guys they would talk later. Since my mom was there in the kitchen, they couldn't talk now. I didn't hear the later discussion, but the same guys he would talk with would eventually show up another day and Leonard would bring them in to watch me rest. After that, Leonard's talk of me with his friends became much looser. We normally got to a point where the conversation would get "too grown up," and I would be excused to go to my room.

I was glad to leave, because I never knew how bad things were going to get. Leonard wasn't violent in the way some people were. He never beat up my mom or destroyed the house. I think he was smarter than most of the other people we were around, but he was very cruel and constantly played mind games. He would push people to a breaking point, then would threaten harm . . . not usually the kind of threat that suggested he would hurt the person directly, but clear threats that he would hurt someone else or make the person hurt someone else. I could barely manage keeping my own mental clarity with him and just couldn't handle watching him play these games with anyone else, especially my mom. So good, I was glad whenever I was excused. It was always my mom who told me to go, so in some way I was glad she did that to get me out of the situation, but even that was unsettling.

When we got to this point, with Leonard having visitors and talking about me, things were getting worse not just with him but also with my mom. She started pulling away and didn't want to talk to Leonard much. She spent most of her time in the kitchen or stayed busy with household tasks and did not spend much time at all visiting when Leonard's friends came by. Then there came the day when he had a couple friends over, my mom was in the kitchen, and I was in my room. Leonard was talking freely about me and describing something about how I looked when I was sleeping.

I had walked out of my room to talk to my mom and saw Leonard mimicking me and how I would lie on my side and move to my back and how that was the best part because he could see my legs start to open. My mom heard me come out from my room and rushed into the front room and scolded Leonard. "Shhh . . . she's right there." Leonard reacted quickly and stopped his story to ask me what I needed.

I responded that I just wanted to talk to my mom, but I was stunned. *Did my mom just stop him from talking about me because I was there? So, she knows? She knew all along?*

I don't even remember what was said after that, but I know I went back to my room and somehow knew that I just got proof that there had been no mistake here: My mom knows what's going on. I put that bit of information away in the back of my head. I couldn't confront her or deal with it now. In fact, I wouldn't really look at it until adulthood, but at the time what I knew was that Mom saw more than she let on, and any sympathy I had for her being stuck with someone she was afraid of was dead. Now I would worry only about me and my brother. Her safety with Leonard was not my concern anymore.

I don't know if it was because her cover was blown, or more likely, because Leonard had started planning some more activity that was beyond even what my mom was willing to go along with. I had always guessed that he would eventually bring one of these other men into the bedroom with us and, frankly, that he was not being as sexual with my mother so she thought she was being replaced. Whatever it was, Leonard was gone very soon.

Jack

After Leonard left, we didn't go straight into the Godly phase, but we did go hard into the drinking phase, which wasn't a big stretch since Mom was already drinking regularly when Leonard was there.

We still had parties, mostly full of drinking and poker games, with lots of strange men around. I tried to make some peace with my mom but knew that eventually we would end up with the same things happening, so I started looking around at who would be the next one and if I had to choose, which one would I be able to deal with best.

Up to this point, I saw that there were some angry and violent men who would physically hurt my mom, but most of those incidents happened when she was out. Maybe it would overflow to when she brought the guy home, but not always. The guys who directly interacted with me were almost always about some kind of sexual experience and a lot of secrecy. There were a few that were what I considered physically dangerous, but most were just disgusting and bothersome. They offended me in their attempt to make me think their advances were all about playing a fun little game and thinking I was too dumb to know what they were doing. There were so many men who just liked sneaking in touches or would lean over to lick me when no one was looking. It was creepy, and honestly, really annoying. But Leonard had been more than that. He was one that was truly dangerous and didn't follow the same limits; he was threatening and didn't have a problem involving other people. I told myself to pay attention because not all men were the same even if they started off with the same actions.

I didn't really know what that meant, because the really dangerous ones didn't come along as often as the creepy touchers, so I didn't have enough practice to figure them out. I did know, though when one of them showed up. I did learn from Leonard that I had to watch out for a lot more than if a guy was going to do something; I had to anticipate what kind of action he would take and how far he would go.

When Jack showed up, he definitely stood out as one I would have to be aware of. I didn't really know how to group him at first: He wasn't exactly like Leonard but was still different and more intimidating than the others. He was angry and wasn't afraid of showing it. When we were at one of the parties with a half dozen other men around, Jack was the one nobody bothered. He could do what he wanted: talk or not talk, ignore people he didn't respect, and fight anyone who wanted to argue with him. The strange part was that he was so much younger than the others but somehow more angry. Jack was in his early twenties, my mom was around forty, and the other men around were generally in their mid-thirties to mid-forties. I don't really know how Jack ended up in this group, but there he was.

Watching him, I saw the one good thing I used to have with Leonard. If I was with him, I would not have to deal with anyone else. Most men don't have the ownership aspect that the more dangerous ones have. Something else stood out—Jack wasn't cruel. He was rageful and violent, but not cruel. All these things made him the best one for me to be next to. It really didn't matter if he attempted to hurt me; most of the guys would in some way. But knowing that it wouldn't be long before someone started up with me, I decided to influence the next move.

It was simple. All I had to do was show him a little more attention and choose my seat to be next to him, so I did. I would talk to him first, offer him food or drinks first, look at him, and show interest. Then I would sit next to him. He always chose a single chair instead of the sofa, so I would sit on the floor. It was clear the choice I was making and when another guy offered an open seat next to him, Jack spoke for me and said I was fine where I was. Good. We agreed then that if anyone was going to approach me, they would have to talk to him.

Jack was different in a few more ways as well. He was angry and bitter but still so young and clearly still trying to figure things out. He had a younger brother who was in his mid- or late teens, and Jack was always fighting with him. I felt sad for them but wasn't really sure why. I thought Jack was really weird with his brother, always mad at him for seemingly no reason. He would explode any time his brother tried to talk to me and was protective of me in an over-the-top way. With his behavior this extreme in protecting me, I honestly expected that he would be worse than Leonard when it finally came time for him to make his move, but I knew that I had made a choice. I would have to handle whatever he was going to do. That was the deal.

I actually tried to create opportunities for him to get on with things. There were several times he was at the house watching us while my mom was out doing things. Roman would be out playing or in the bedroom, and I would choose to stay with Jack so I could keep up my side of the agreement. Nothing. Jack never made a move but always wanted me to stay with him so he would know that no one else was bothering me. In a way I felt very safe, because I really believed that if he saw anyone attempt to approach me, he would do what he could to stop it. In this, though, I didn't exactly feel comfortable. I felt somehow heartbroken. This guy was deeply angry, deeply sad, and seemed to want someone to protect; I just didn't know why.

One night, Jack and his brother were there. I don't recall all of the circumstances that led up to it, but at some point, Jack was in the front room and his brother was in the bedroom. His brother called me in and told me to lock the door. When I went in, I saw him lying in bed in his underwear, masturbating. Then I suddenly knew why Jack was so angry and why he and his brother were always fighting. I saw that Jack was asking the same kinds of questions I was. Obviously they had both been sexually abused growing up, and Jack was struggling with the question of how people start off as children not abusing people and then somewhere along the line become abusive themselves. Looking at this situation, I knew that Jack was screaming and fighting to try not to repeat the same pattern, but his brother was not. Once again, I had a choice to make, stay or leave. It was clear what this was going to be about, but Jack was right outside and I didn't feel any real fear. I wanted to know why he was doing this. So I stayed and locked the door as I was told.

He seemed satisfied that I had followed his direction and told me to join him in bed. Then he kept touching himself and started describing how he liked oral sex to be performed. I watched him with a sense of disappointment and sadness. Why was he doing this? It can't be because he doesn't know any better. Even if he didn't, his brother had clearly pointed out that this was the wrong decision to make. So I asked him, "Why are you doing this?"

He answered that it just feels good and kept rubbing himself. "No." I made it clear I wasn't talking about masturbation. I repeated the question in a way he knew I wasn't going to change the subject. "Why are you doing this?" He knew what I was asking but didn't want to answer.

He just said that if I didn't want to play, he could make me. I was still standing near the door and responded by telling him I could also unlock the door and call his brother. That made him change his tone, and his voice became somewhat pleading. "No, please don't open the door. You don't have to play."

I looked at him very closely and told myself to pay attention. This is how it happens. He is just learning how to do this and he isn't sure how. I saw what I thought was a confused child who needed someone to clear up his head. I wasn't mad at him; I was disgusted with the world. I also noticed how scared he was with the threat of his brother finding out what he was doing. That meant he had tried this before. That's why Jack was so protective of me. He didn't want to become a sexual abuser and wanted to do whatever he could to keep his brother from becoming one.

I let him off the hook and told him I wasn't going to call Jack in, but I was going to unlock the door and leave the room. I didn't say anything to Jack, but I got that if Jack did do something to me it wouldn't be sexual. I had a new respect for him because of that but wasn't sure how I was going to handle any other kind of attack.

The night it finally happened, it was late. I don't know where my mom was—probably on a date or across the street drinking with the neighbor. Jack was at our house and was already pissed off. Something had happened, but I never found out exactly what it was. My guess was that something happened with him and his dad, but who knows. The one thing that was clear was that he was past his limit, and I saw why people didn't mess with him when he was angry. But this was the time for me not to leave him but to stay close. This was the time for me to keep my side of the deal and stick around.

He was pacing and talking to himself, arguing to the air. He threw something toward me while he was yelling. I ducked down out of the way and started quietly crying. I didn't even really listen to what he was saying; I knew it wasn't about me. He was just yelling out arguments. I was afraid but tried to keep myself together and watch him. Partly to see if his next move was going to be directly at me so I could run, but more because I wanted to see if he was still there—actually present enough to know what was going on. Or would he go away like Mom did?

No, he was talking to someone who wasn't there, but he didn't fade out. He was clearly still present. Between his yelling and random punching of the walls and furniture, he would look at me. When he did, I tried to keep eye contact to let him know I was still there. I wasn't going to leave him, but instead of giving him any comfort, it seemed to make him angrier.

He would look at me, keep eye contact, and then punch the wall. After a couple times, I saw that the eye contact was too much, so I changed to looking at his face but not his eyes. He ranted a little longer and knocked himself against the wall. Then it just stopped, and he started crying. I stayed cowering down against the wall and looked at him. I was glad he hadn't hit me directly and knew that when he looked at me he was trying to keep his head together.

The event was scary, but I knew that this was my place and this was what I would have to take if I were to keep looking for him to protect me. And somehow, after everything that night, what I wanted was to just stay in the moment of stillness and honesty when he finally stopped being so angry. I wanted to be able to just look at him through the eyes of the young girl that I was and have him look back at me to acknowledge that we were the same—neither of us know what we are supposed to do. He did look at me, and I believe he was acknowledging everything that I was thinking. I don't remember the rest of the night except that I went to bed not telling anyone what happened but knowing that Jack had showed me something that I would have to learn from.

It is strange because I had not experienced moments of such raw honesty and vulnerability with the men who were more sexual in their approach. With Jack, and later with other men, I saw that it was the really angry ones who seemed to hold some sense of clarity underneath their rage that allowed some space to acknowledge that the distortion was too much for even them to hold. And when that time came, I was somehow on equal footing and could see him clearly. My sight called him out as being as afraid and uncertain as I was. When I first saw this with Jack, I understood that this is what people work for . . . whatever it takes, find a place past the noise and hold the honesty of what is in front of you. This is a hard space to find. I had guessed that I was beginning to understand why my mom kept getting hurt. My question now is if that meant people have to be violent first to allow this to happen or is it possible to reveal a deeper self without hurting one another? Isn't there a way without the rage? This question, I've spent years trying to answer.

The Offering

The following months were full of loud parties, lots of alcohol, and random men showing up either at the block party or directly at our place. We had a lot of nights when conflicts would get too intense, and my mom would tell one of the neighbors to watch me and my brother in the house. Sometimes she would get hit, sometimes not. Sometimes she'd come back with some guy, sometimes not. Either way, there were lots of nights where my mom was so drunk, she would collapse on the kitchen floor and either pass out or throw up all over the place, and I would always go in to make sure she was okay and to clean up. I hated the sound of her voice calling me—the loud and slurred speech with drool running down her chin and neck. I hated her smell and hated having to try to get her cleaned up and to bed.

I would argue with my mom a lot, challenging her on why, again, are we still doing this? I challenged her with questions like why she kept drinking when she knew that things were worse when she did. I remember a night I refused to help her up and told her she could just pass out and sleep where she was. It made things worse when she argued back about how hard it was to have kids and take care of us, but she still did it. I remember a hard argument one day when she talked about how difficult it was to have us, so I yelled at her and asked her why then, exactly, did she have kids? Was it to have someone to mop up after she threw up or to have someone to spank and laugh at when she got mad? She yelled back and kept saying she was my mother, and this wasn't why she had kids.

I picked up a knife and kept asking her, why then? To give her boyfriends someone to grab onto? I kept yelling with the knife in my hand. I think I scared her, and I was glad. I wanted her to wake up. I had an impulse to cut myself in an attempt to scream louder, to show her something that was clear enough to make her see that something was wrong here. Why was she not seeing this? Instead, I grabbed a bunch of my hair and cut part of it. That ended the argument that day and somehow got her attention. We talked a little after and I told her that I was tired of all of her boyfriends and strange visitors always touching or kissing me. She said she didn't know they all did that. We did not talk specifically about Leonard or how she knew what he had done with me, but she told me after that she wouldn't let things like that happen again with anyone else.

Things didn't change a lot after I cut my hair, but I did see that in some ways she made attempts to listen to me when I spoke. I tried to pull back and stop challenging her and tried to trust that she would protect me better. The test came soon enough when one of her friends did it again. "Two-toes" was what he called himself; he had his big toe and two small toes cut off of his left foot. He talked about how a lot of black men had their toes cut, because it made it harder for them to run. The two middle toes were kept so they could still walk and work. I never knew his real name, but he was one of the men my mom welcomed into our place several times after Leonard. Two-toes would talk about how much a man needs to respect a woman and told my mom that Leonard was not a real man with how he had acted. Then, of course, he also made his advance on me, put his hand between my legs, and told me that we would wait until my mom went to sleep. He said he wasn't going to be like Leonard; he would treat me right.

We were getting to a place where some of the noise was settling down. We didn't have so many people coming by and not so many parties—and this guy was overall a nice one. He wasn't rude, he showed gratitude when my mom made food, he was generally polite, but now here we are with the usual move. And I am going to be the one to say something that will create problems again. I'm tired and don't want to deal with this.

I had to again redirect my thinking. I had a chance to make a different decision than I did with Nino. I didn't trust my mom then, and things kept happening. So maybe now if she really does want to know and really will do something, then I should deal with it and figure out how to tell her. So I waited until Two-toes wasn't there before I talked to her. I started by reminding her that we had said we were doing things differently, so I would now tell her when someone tried to touch me. Then I told her about Two-toes. I acknowledged that he was always nice, and I knew she liked him, but yes, he did approach me. I again reminded her that she had said she wanted me to say something, but she seemed disappointed. I assumed it was because she trusted that he wouldn't do this, but part of me thought she was just tired too. She said she wanted me to speak up, but really, no one would want to have this problem handed off to them. She listened and took what I said, told me that it was good that I said something, and that she would deal with it.

She didn't say anything else, which made me a little nervous, but I told myself that I would have to let her deal with it and not push her to tell me anything. We soon went across the street to this lady's place where we would sometimes go when my mom was having a hard time. While we were there, I heard my mom talk to her about what I had said. I wasn't supposed to be listening, so I didn't try to hear the whole conversation. But I heard enough to worry that I would not be able to just trust that my mom would handle it.

Two-toes had been gone during this time. He went to the market to get drinks, but he was going to be back soon. In the meantime, my mom drank—a lot. The more she drank, the angrier she got. The conversation between her and the neighbor lady became very intense, but I couldn't tell at first what was going on in the discussion. Eventually my mom went back across to our place, but my brother and I were told to stay with the neighbor and to go into the bedroom. Before she left, I heard enough to know that my mom's plan was to wait for Two-toes with a kitchen knife. I heard the neighbor lady tell her not to do it, that it was a bad decision. I remembered what happened last time my mom got a knife, back when we were with Fred. Tonight was going to be like that night.

I was right in my assumption. She was going to try to "teach him a lesson." I watched from the bedroom window and saw that Two-toes had come back, and I started hearing loud and hard fighting. I heard yelling and saw neighbors starting to react, coming out to see what was happening. The fight was in our place, so no one could see how far things were going. I was scared and mad. This is how she's going to handle it? Kill him, get arrested, and leave me and Roman with the neighbor? How is that protecting me or my brother— and how am I supposed to trust a killer, even if she is my mother? No, I am not going to watch this happen, and I am not going to make my brother visit our mother in jail. So for the second time, I went to the phone and dialed zero to call the police to come before my mom went too far. I told them my mom was fighting a man and she had a knife. The police were there very quickly and then the whole neighborhood was out watching, just like last time.

I guess my mom did attack Two-toes during the argument, but the fight was broken up before anyone got hurt beyond recovery. There were a lot of police there, and Roman and I were taken back to our place after they arrived. I hated my mom for putting us in this situation. All of these strange men, the same things happening over and over again, and her answer was always to fight, which meant I had to figure things out. Now here we are in the middle of this, having to talk to the police. I remember it was a female officer who came to talk with me and Roman. I don't remember everything, but I do remember her telling me that she knew what the man had done and she knew what my mom did. She was very kind in how she spoke to me but still came from a place of strength, as if she was telling me I didn't have to prove anything and she could do something about it. It made me feel a little better for a minute, long enough to stop worrying and really look at her. She had dark hair, long I think, but it was tied up and pinned under her hat. She looked at me directly— no side glances or split attention. She asked me if things like this happened a lot. Before I said anything I'm sure my expression provided the answer, because my thought was, "Yes. All the time, but what does that mean? Will you take my mom away?" I think she saw my response. In answer she said, "Because if it does, we can help make it stop."

I had a rush of thoughts when I heard that. I was so angry with my mom, I didn't care what happened to her. Jail? Fine. Taken away from me? Fine. Let her go! She keeps telling me how bad her life is anyway, so take her. Then I thought of my brother and was afraid of what that would mean for him. Just because I am ready to have Mom taken away doesn't mean he is. And what about us? If they take Mom, will they pull me and Roman apart? That cannot happen—I cannot let

that happen. I looked at Roman and saw real fe
eyes.

"No," I answered the lady officer.

I think she knew I was making a decision and
offered me another chance. "Are you sure this is the
only time this happened?"

"Yes, this is the only time."

At the end of the night, Two-toes had been
taken away and Mom stayed. I knew I had made
another decision to just stay and take it and thought
that my mistake this time was speaking up. I was right
the first time with Nino. My fears of what would really
happen were valid. I said something and it wasn't worth
it. I could have lost my brother and seen my mother
with a dead man's blood on her. And the whole thing
became about how hard my mom's life was with no
discussion of what kept happening to her kids. The
lesson here was not to keep looking for Mom to protect
me. I had told myself before that she was not capable;
I had to learn to accept that and just figure things out
myself. What's important is me and Roman.

I think things were getting to my mom. We were
having too many hard arguments, she was drinking
insanely, and her seven-year-old daughter had again
called her out and had the police come to keep her from
creating too many problems. It was time to go and start
again somewhere else. Soon after the police incident,
we were headed out of California to Oklahoma to
reconnect and get some help from the family.

Part Three:
Unreasonable Responsibility

Walking on the sand, the sun is bright, or it seems it should be.

I am young, maybe six, wearing a plain white gown and nothing on my feet.
The sky is clear, it's mid-day, I can hear the ocean and feel the sand
under my feet.

It's not bright, though.
It's dull, almost grey, like everything has a mold growing on it.

There is trash everywhere. Lots of glass liquor bottles and rubbish that seemed to be just thrown around.

I feel defeated. I know my job here is to clean up but I don't understand why no one is here, and this is not my trash.

I walk very carefully toward the water. I want to feel the coolness on my feet and see the clear beauty of the water before I start cleaning up.

*I reach the water and see
the endlessness of the ocean,
clear and overwhelming.*

*The waves wash up a medicine bottle.
It was clean and had no cloudy
greyness to it.*

*I picked it up and felt some
recognition and relief.*

*It was the same medicine my mom used at
home –
her cure-all for whatever ails her.*

*It reminds me that I haven't seen her.
Where is she?*

Oklahoma

It took us about a day and half on the Greyhound to make it to Chickasha. I remember looking out the window into the darkness as we drove through long spans of empty dessert. It was a little scary to look out and see almost complete darkness. I'd really work to find something recognizable and would remind myself that there was still life all around when I found some kind of cactus or other strange plant I had not seen before. That was something Mom would remind me to do when things were scary—look for life. If someone looks too big or frightening, look them in the eyes and find the person behind the scars and tattoos or strange clothes. If you think you're alone, look for the trees or the birds or other living things to remind yourself you're not.

I still don't know what to think about our time in Oklahoma. Mom was good at talking up the chance to start over. I think she knew the arguments we had were about real problems that she had no way of fixing, and we both needed some space for the hope of things getting better, so she would talk a lot about simple comforts that we would enjoy this time. She would talk about what could happen, how things could be better in our new home. We would have new, clean beds with new sheets, we would put our clothes away in new drawers, and we'd cook together and eat in our new home. Things would be better this time. I wanted to believe her, but it was hard. How many times can we start over and still feel hopeful about it?

And as much as I think we both wanted to hold some comfort in each other, somehow things were changing between me and my mom. I wasn't sure how we would recover from Barstow . . . how could I really look to my mom with a trust that she will love and protect me after what just happened? And how could my mom expect me to follow her lead without question? Things were unbalanced for a long time, but now it seemed we were both too exposed and too vulnerable to just keep going, though I didn't know what it meant if we didn't figure out how to do just that.

Moving back to see family was a last resort, but I think Mom felt at this point there really was nothing else that seemed an option. I didn't know how many things had happened to create the kinds of problems my mom had with the rest of the family but until we were actually going to visit them, I wasn't even aware that any family connection existed. When we did talk about it, Mom said there was one aunt that would help us. Then we would just have to see what happens.

Like the other places, we weren't in Chickasha long—maybe a year. When we first arrived, we spent some time living with Aunt Beth. Old and kind-hearted, she was fair, almost completely white in color, with random age spots on her hands and face and never-ending layers of loose, baggy skin. Beth was the only aunt my mom seemed to trust. Beth was the one my mom reached out to and the one I guessed knew things about my mom's life, so there wasn't the sense of secrecy around her that was often there when Mom started talking about family. Beth showed a lot of affection and gave my mom time to rest. I think it was a relief for my mom to be there for a little while.

We didn't have much money, so housing options were limited but Mom did eventually find a little corner house with one real bedroom in the back, past the kitchen, and an attic that could be turned into two kid bedrooms. It was small, but good for what we needed, and very cheap. It wasn't until a few months later when we found out why it was so much less than every other place: It was the only house in the neighborhood without a cellar. Being an L.A. native, I never even knew why that was important until tornado season came around. Luckily, there was only one that threatened our home, and the man who lived across the street called us over to take shelter with him until it passed.

I think we tried, again, to be normal. Mom wasn't drinking so much and didn't really date. We did go back to God again but in a different way. There was a neighborhood church we often went to that was just a short walk down the street. I don't know what kind of church it was. I know it was Christian based, but certainly not Catholic. The church itself was very simple—not a lot of artistic windows or statues. And in this one there was no holy water at the entrance. The music was different too. Almost everything, in fact, was different. The Christian sermons were similar in meaning, but the delivery was much more dramatic. Church would go on for hours, the preachers seemed to speak with their whole bodies, and vocal tones and volumes were all over the place. I could see, if someone were to choose a church to attend, how this would certainly keep your attention. Especially after the main sermon, when it was time for sharing, people would testify about some key lesson or blessing they wanted to share. Then somehow, when there was enough excitement, someone would speak in tongues. Then another person from across the room would translate the message. Then, eventually, the singing would start. I was glad Mom had the church; I always thought she needed a way to cry and scream, and I was glad it wasn't by my bedside.

We went on for a few months at the little house. Roman and I went to school; I was in second grade. I did well with my schoolwork and had a little boyfriend. I liked Scottie so much it made me sad. Sad because I knew I would not be with him long and I knew it was just a matter of time before things would start happening again. I didn't want Scottie to see any of that, and I wasn't sure if it was me causing it. Something happened to me from going through so many incidents with creepy, scary men, something that felt like a poison that I wouldn't be able to get out of my body. I couldn't be sure, but if it was something in me, then either I was born with it or I somehow got it later. I couldn't understand it, but I didn't want to take the chance of infecting him if it was possible that my fears were true.

I would spend time and enjoy Scottie's attention, but I would also talk very seriously about how one day I would go away and it would be good because bad things sometimes happen and it would be better if I was gone when they did. Scottie was such a sweet boy. He would listen to my fears but never wanted to think that what I said was true. When he asked me to marry him, I remember being so clear in my thoughts of being responsible and not promising a future to someone I care about when I knew it was a lie. I told him we would likely not even grow up together and that later he would find a different girl to marry. I told him that would be good because then maybe he wouldn't see some of the bad things. But he kept asking me and eventually qualified his proposal, asking if we were still together and we still loved each other, then would I then marry him after we finish school? "Yes," I told him and actually meant it. *If by some miracle I am here, and you know about the bad things and you still love me, then yes, we will get married.* Pretty serious discussion for second graders, but I promised myself I would not be one of those women who would lie about things to get what they want.

At home Mom and I tried to get along, both doing what we were supposed to do. I did chores and got my first babysitting job watching the houseful of kids for the neighbor when she and my mom visited and went for groceries. Mom would try to encourage me to draw and keep some sense of playfulness around Christmas.

Our efforts may have helped, but it was as though there was already too much or not enough done or said. I knew why I was angry and disappointed with my mom, but I couldn't understand why she was so angry and disappointed with me. She didn't talk about it but seemed to quietly stew. It would come up when I would misbehave or intentionally make a choice to voice a disagreement. She would react in what I thought was an extreme way—just too angry and determined to make some kind of point. I would ask her why she was so mad at me. I had challenged her before when she would spank me with what seemed to be more of a rage than an attempt to teach and discipline. Even while she spanked me, I would keep challenging her, asking why she was so mad and hateful. She didn't give an explanation, so I would keep guessing and asking.

Did she enjoy hitting me? If she didn't, then she would have to stop these games of trying to sneak up and "get me." I also accused her of trying to trap me so she could hit me longer. She would start telling me to repeat things she had said to me. I would sometimes try but then would not get the words right, and she would use that as an excuse to keep punishing me. I told her that if she just wanted to hit me, she should be honest about it and not try to trick me into saying something she knew I would get wrong. Then, it's just her pretending that I deserve it when she is just mad. I had started challenging her like this back at Fred's place. When she would say that the spankings hurt her more than they did me. I'd ask her why she always laughed and told other people how funny it was. If it hurt her so much, then she wouldn't think it was such a fun game.

We had an argument like that one night in the little house, and I told her I would take as many spankings as she wanted to give me if she could just tell me why I deserved so many. This is another lesson I learned: just asking the question forces some consideration, even if no direct answer is voiced. It's a risky approach, because the listener may just blow up and things could get worse, but since this wasn't the first time I would point things out to her I expected that she would either hear me or I would run faster than her. That night, the argument gave her a moment of pause and I didn't have to run.

My spankings all but completely stopped after that. I think there may have been one more attempt, but when my mom looked at me and knew I was not just showing up to take my punishment but instead was questioning if she was teaching me something or just being mean, the interaction became too honest, so it stopped.

***

Some other things were going on while we were in the little house. I was starting to get sick. I had a couple of occasions of long-lasting fevers, and several periods of exhaustion. I slept a lot and seemed to scare easily. I had lots of nightmares and sometimes just froze in the middle of doing things. I spent a lot of time wondering what was next and how I would take care of myself when I was in the world trying to create my own life. I thought about death a lot. This time I'd know better about what to do to make sure it worked. I would spend time on the plan but decided I would not take action unless there was no other way out and I knew how to say good-bye to Roman. I took comfort in knowing that if things got too bad I'd be able to do something about it.

It was in the little house where we learned about our other siblings. Mom had talked about having other kids just a few times in the past but not with a lot of details. Now we are learning that besides me and Roman, there are five others that are thought to still be alive and seven others that had died either at or shortly after birth.

Wayne was Mom's first child. She said that *they* had taken him from her, that her mother knew him but did not want them to be in touch. Mom didn't know where the others were or if anyone in the family knew them. She talked a little about mean, dangerous men she had once been with—no real detail of what *mean* or *dangerous* meant, but from her tone and with what I had already seen, I believed that the words were appropriate. When she talked, I felt that she was showing me something about her life that she didn't know how to explain. What I heard was her telling me again that this is just how things are, that she had known many men and most were dangerous and she had never seen a way to get away from that truth. I remember looking at her with mixed feelings . . . some sense of compassion and sadness, but with another fighting drive telling me that this can't be the only way.

I wanted to focus on something more hopeful. It was exciting to know that I had another brother that was out in the world somewhere. And not just out roaming around wondering what to do, but with a wife he loved and had created a life with. Mom got a picture of Wayne, a shot of this young man standing in front of a home with his wife.

I would talk to him in the picture and would tell him I was happy he made it out. I told him that I'd keep trying, and one day I would be out too. I told him I was happy he found a pretty lady for his wife and that I wouldn't tell her about the bad things; she didn't need to know all this stuff. I would be embarrassed for him or his wife to know me in the life that I had at the time. But I promised that if I could make it out, that he would be proud of me. Then maybe, if he wanted, we could meet.

***

I liked the little house, but Mom kept looking around and found what she thought would be a good move. There was a cheap house not far away that was for sale, and she somehow figured out a way to get us in. I never knew the details on how it worked out, since our sole income was her disability check, but she got things together and we moved in. It was a real fixer-upper with two stories, but there was too much damage on the second floor, so we weren't allowed to go upstairs. My mom, though, was very handy. She had learned to prove herself doing "man's work" with odd jobs throughout her years and was not afraid of physical labor, so it felt like a real win for her to be in a position to own a home, no matter how much work it needed.

When we moved to the big house, Roman and I shared the front bedroom by separating space with a sheet hung on a wire across the middle of the room. The property had a guest house in the back yard that Mom soon rented out to a young couple.

The big house never really felt like home, and it turned out to be a short stay for us—just a few months through the summer. Having a chance to own a home seemed to be a marker of success for my mom, so I was hoping that she would start to feel more excited. Instead, she would go between seeming okay and then back to heavy drinking binges. I wasn't sure what exactly happened at the time, but she was talking more to her mother and learning more about Wayne's life, so it seemed that maybe connections would be rebuilt.

Eventually, we did get to meet her mom and brother when they came for a short visit. Roman and I were excited to meet family but remembered that the connection between Mom and the others was the first thing that needed to be tested. If that connection didn't work, then there was no hope we would ever build a new one. The first visit was very short. They were in town to see other family and saw us while they were there, then they went back home to California. Mom seemed to be glad that there was some communication, but I think it was far from what she wanted. We went on just a little while longer, then something happened. Mom said she got a call that her mother was sick, so we packed up and headed to Ventura.

Mom had befriended the young couple renting the guest house and had told them that if we didn't come back in a couple months, then they could take over the payments and the house would be theirs. Needless to say, we didn't return. I hope the house turned out to be a good thing for them.

Ventura

We moved to Ventura and at first stayed with Grandma and Uncle David. David was in his mid-thirties but still lived at home due to his mental development limitations. *Retarded* was the term used then, and it wasn't a slur, it simply meant that mental progress had been stifled. Mom loved her brother and would build him up whenever she could. Mom felt that David's limited development was a direct result of the physical abuse and humiliation that her mother had inflicted and allowed.

My mom didn't get along well with her mother. I think she loved her mom and was intensely hurt that her mother was not very loving toward her. I learned that my mom had been on her own or floating among foster homes most of her youth and that there was a lot of physical and sexual abuse as she grew up. Things that I had no hesitation believing, even though from the outside, most people saw my grandmother as a kind Christian woman who took care of her challenged son and opened her home to her estranged daughter and grandkids. I knew what it was like to have outsiders look and think everything was okay. People looked at our little family and thought things were just fine, that my mom was a great mother with well-behaved kids to prove it. Things actually started to make more sense after I saw Mom in her own mother's company. If she grew up like this, then maybe she never knew anyone who wasn't violent or mean-hearted.

Still, with more insight and some sense of compassion for her past, I continued to question things. In a way, I held my mom to a higher standard. If she knew how bad things hurt kids, then why would she have her own kids deal with the same things? A question I would never directly ask her just because I didn't really want to challenge her life with her mom. Looking at whatever happened between the two of them was my mom's job, not mine. I had to stick with just us—that was enough. As I grew up, I saw that my mom did try to avoid making some of the same mistakes her mom had. That's why she always encouraged questioning and always hugged and kissed us good night. Her mother was very shaming when my mom needed affection or asked about things she didn't understand. Those two things specifically my mom made clear efforts to change for us.

***

The first place we found in Ventura was just within a mile of Grandma's home, a small green duplex with a yard overgrown with grass and weeds. Amy was the neighbor lady next door that my mom befriended. She had two older kids, Sheila and Edgar. Amy was kind to us but clearly had problems bringing up her kids; both were incredibly angry and found ways to act out.

Sheila was seventeen, I think. Her boyfriend, Daryl, was in his twenties. He was a creepy guy who started openly touching me, but it seemed we were at a point where Mom didn't pretend to know or not know anymore; it was just there. Edgar was eighteen and extremely angry with his mom, but he seemed to take to my mom and was very good to me and to Roman. I hated when Sheila showed up, because Daryl always tagged along. Edgar, though, I was always glad to see. He seemed to be aware enough of his own anger and wanted to do something with his life to overcome the things he had learned. I wasn't clear on the things that had happened, but I was encouraged that here was another example of someone who was trying to be better than what he was taught.

I think Edgar helped to make Ventura a good place for Roman; I am happy about that. For me, Ventura was a terrible place. There was a lot of discovery there—not exciting, promising discovery, but other important things that forced me to take clear and decisive positions about my life.

By the time we got to Ventura, Mom was heavy into her drinking again, and I was sick a lot. I started missing some school back in Oklahoma, because I kept getting these episodes of what seemed like blackouts followed by hours of exhaustion. We were in the green duplex when I was diagnosed with petit mall epilepsy. I didn't drop and shake during seizures but would seem to lose connection with my surroundings and sometimes would just get up and start walking away. Or if I had something in my hand, I would start moving my arm in a stabbing or scribbling motion. Then

I'd become aware again but would have no recollection of what had just happened. Mom said I had these incidents since I was a very young girl, but they had gotten worse and more frequent. It wasn't until this point that a doctor finally witnessed an incident and diagnosed me.

The seizures themselves generally lasted just a few minutes, but the effects were exhausting. There was a period when I would have a three- or four-minute seizure and then would have to sleep three or four hours to recover. I'd wake up still drained, and after a couple hours, I'd have another seizure and sleep more. I missed a lot of third grade because of this.

The days I did get to school, I enjoyed. I was considered an advanced learner and had a great teacher who would find different ways to help me develop outside the standard lesson plans. She had set up a lot of things for me. I was partnered with other students to help them learn, I got to go to the advanced class once a week, and I had a math tutor come in to meet with me. It felt good to have someone show me that I didn't have to hide myself for being smart, but I could have a place in the group like everyone else; I needed to be shown that.

I loved my teacher and felt a little scared that she would no longer trust me to do more after she learned of my diagnosis. I felt extremely embarrassed after she first saw me in a seizure. I had walked up to her in the middle of class, leaned up against her as though I was about to hug her, and then just walked away. I didn't remember any part of that, but eventually felt myself walking and started looking around for the classroom I thought I was in. Then I stopped and looked around and saw that I was outdoors and had walked out of class and down the walkway headed out of the school. When I saw that my teacher had followed me and watched me, I started crying, thinking she wouldn't like me anymore and wondering how I was going to explain this. I was so relieved and honestly didn't quite know what to think when she just comforted me and didn't show any signs of being mad or afraid.

It was after this event when my mom had the official talk with the principal and my teacher to explain my condition. It was also my best example of how to manage it. My teacher took the information, asked some questions about what to expect, and then shared it with the class in a way that just said this was something for us to know in case a seizure came up. No fear, no apologies, no punishments—just acknowledging a part of me. That was the second thing she gave me that I really needed.

***

We had been on a waiting list to get a place in a low-income housing project nearby, and it was just a few months before we got approval to move in. Amy got in first, and we got a unit close to hers. Ours was the only single unit, all the way at the end of the lot.

Mom started dating again, and the parties started up more frequently. We went through a few instances of long-lasting Bible reviews and kneeling prayers, but that didn't last long. Mom went more with a lot of drinking and dating.

Things got a lot worse with the men. I hated when Daryl came by. His sexual actions were more and more obvious. He would put his hands between my legs and try to stick his tongue in my mouth when he "said hello," but it was never objected to even when my mom was right there, even when Sheila was there. My mom started coming to me more often after her dates, sitting on my bed, drunk and talking about her dates and her sexual past. I had gotten to where I just listened and stopped asking questions. There was no point when she was drunk. She couldn't hear me no matter what I would ask or say I needed. She would, though, acknowledge that I was just a kid and shouldn't have to listen to adult problems, but I was the only one she had. And I already knew things, so she knew I understood some of what she was talking about.

Mom and I went through ups and downs in our communication. We kept trying, and it sometimes seemed we'd progress, but it's hard to build on things when there are still unspoken realities affecting us.

Mom found a guy she liked enough to date more than once and eventually had him over for dinner at the house to meet us. This was an important night. Mom needed someone in her life to be excited about, and this was the first date she had at home since the police incident in Barstow.

She let me know that she wanted this dinner to go well and reminded me to be polite. She didn't have to say anything; I already knew this was important not just for her but for us. Things couldn't have gone more wrong with Leonard, and I didn't want to do anything to mess things up this time. I wanted to show my mom that I wanted her to be happy. Mom didn't dress up often, but when she did, it seemed to both feel good for her and also put some pressure on her. I made a point to tell her how nice she looked and helped her get the table set.

I don't remember what we served, and don't really remember her date. What I remember is trying to do everything right and not embarrass my mom. I smiled and was polite. I helped with serving and clearing and didn't talk too much. I said "yes, sir" and "no, sir" and tried to stay out of the way. Mom seemed to enjoy how things were going, and her date thanked her for a good dinner.

It was when we were clearing the table and her date was thanking me for all the work I had done to help when it happened. He was still sitting at the table and called me over to give me a proper "thank you." He put his arm around me and started rubbing my thighs, then leaned in to kiss my neck. I tightened up and tried to quickly figure out what the best move would be. *Do I stand here and let him keep touching me? Is Mom watching? She hasn't said anything and just walked a few steps to the kitchen behind us, so maybe she doesn't know? I can't tell.* She came back and his arm was still around me with his hand on my butt. I pulled away and kept clearing dishes. My mom didn't make a scene, but I think she saw what happened. They stayed at the table and talked a while. I heard him tell my mom how mature I was but then I went into the bedroom, so I wouldn't hear more or do anything that would make him call me over again. I stayed out of the way until he was gone.

When he left, my mom let me know that she saw what I was doing and how I made him want me. She was so angry, because she really liked this one. She didn't care about the others, but why did I have to always take the ones she liked? I remember that night all too well. I was hurt and angry—angry that she still blamed me for Leonard, which was bad enough, but she wouldn't actually say his name or admit that her accusation tonight was really about her thinking I took Leonard from her. And the guy tonight . . . why isn't she mad at him? He put his hands on me and clearly wanted more, but I walked away. I didn't do anything to make him touch me, and I didn't ask him to keep going; I left. What else was I supposed to do?

She said again that she saw me trying to make him like me. I reminded her that she told me to be polite, and I was. That's all. It felt like she hated me and held an anger that would never fade, but I think she was also too tired to go through the fight. She finally seemed to give up and told me in that terrible "I'm-just-so-disappointed" voice that even if I didn't mean it, it really was me that made men do this. It wasn't anything I did exactly, it's just me . . . something that they want, something that invites them . . . something that not every woman has, but I do and I keep showing it.

I stopped arguing and listened to what she was saying. *A woman? Aren't I still a girl? I guess that doesn't matter if I'm doing something wrong here.* I started thinking of all the times she would get upset at how I looked: my hair down was too attractive, my hair up showed my neck and was too seductive, skirts just invited touches, pants showed too much of my shape—whatever I did seemed to be a problem with how I looked. Is that what she was talking about? It didn't make sense, because at the same time, Mom constantly asked people to forgive how I looked because of my weight. None of this seemed right, but I knew she was telling me something that I had to pay attention to and try to understand.

I didn't try to tell her it wasn't me but instead asked what this meant. "What do I have to do to make it different?" She explained that there is nothing I can do to change it. I have to just make a decision about what kind of woman I would be. Women who have this either become whores who sell themselves and take other women's men, or they learn respect and leave other women's men alone. So far I was a whore and had to figure out how to be something else.

I wanted to believe that there was a mistake. I wanted to tell myself that there's no way what my mom was saying could be true, but her explanation did make sense. Why else would this keep happening? Everywhere we moved, a new place with new people, still I find the same thing happening to me. It's not like I ask for it, but whatever it was, I couldn't get away from it. This night I started to wonder if she was right. If she was, this was my responsibility, and I would have to make some decisions very quickly.

***

We got through that night and again tried to just keep going. I kept the information in my head and would try to find some way to either prove, or hopefully, disprove my mom's belief that it was my fault that so many men kept coming to me. I was careful not to show any interest in anyone, kept quiet about my thoughts and interests, and just kept to myself and did what I was supposed to do.

Though I did what I thought I needed to do so I could keep myself hidden, one thing I couldn't help was the fact that I developed early. I was eight years old and already well developed in my bust and had just recently started my period. Mom had talked to me for a while about how girls develop and how it is all part of the maturity of life that one day grows into a relationship, marriage, and eventually children. We had started talking about where babies come from back at Fred's place, just before I started school. I got the mechanics but was too young to even begin to understand the full explanation my mom was giving me. She would tell me that I didn't have to remember everything, but one day, things would make sense after my body had a chance to grow up. I always wanted to know things right away, but the way she explained it, I understood there was simply nothing more that could be said. I would just have to wait.

I remember it was in Ventura when the day finally came. I was in the bedroom changing clothes. I was close to my period and feeling changes. My breasts were sore and swollen; I was a little uncomfortable but somehow excited about everything. I was thinking about what was happening and started to think of all the things my mom had told me about how wonderful it is for girls to grow into being women and how amazing pregnancy was. I suddenly started thinking that something good was happening to me. All the things Mom had talked about were real. Maybe this means I would someday be pregnant and get to feel a baby growing in me. I was so excited and wanted to get my mom and tell her that things were finally making sense.

Right then, as I was putting on my bra, Edgar opened the door and was about to walk through to the bathroom. The interruption broke my train of thought, and I quickly turned my head to the door. He paused as he looked at me, and I saw something in his face. Then he apologized and closed the door as he walked out. As I stood there, I suddenly had a completely different understanding of what was happening. I got what my mom was trying to tell me the night of our last argument: *It is me.* Even Edgar saw it; that's why he walked out. I didn't do anything, I didn't say anything, but still he saw something and it made him leave. It was then I decided that all my excitement about maybe one day having babies would have to be put to sleep. If I do have something in me that I can't help having and it brings these terrible things to me, just like mom said, then there is no question here—I will *never* have babies. What if I have a daughter and whatever this is that is in me is in her, too? I can't tell my baby it is her fault that people keep hurting her, and I won't be able to always protect her. Excitement turned to shame and fear very quickly. Fantasies of one day being a mother are over.

When I came out of the room, Edgar was on the sofa and called me over and asked me to sit next to him. He spoke very caringly and told me that he knew I was growing up, and he would never walk in without knocking again. Edgar handled the whole situation perfectly and in another life this could have been a very encouraging experience. With what I had already learned, though, this was an acknowledgment that I couldn't control whatever was in me that would get a different kind of attention: I had to be clear in my decision that whatever happened, I would not bring a child into this insanity.

***

All of these things were taking a toll on me. I was becoming intensely depressed and by this time had a full blown binge eating disorder. No one called it that then, and my mom only talked about my weight as a shameful detail about her daughter that she asked people to forgive, but I had made the decision back at Fred's place that I would do anything to keep from having to be a violent alcoholic. So I always went to eat when Mom tried to get me to drink or if I knew I would have to keep from crying. By the time we were in Ventura, I actually recognized that I didn't know how to keep from screaming other than very, very quickly binging.

The seizures were also getting much worse; I started fourth grade just before my ninth birthday but by now had all but completely stopped going to school and was regularly fighting to keep myself awake and clearheaded. We had tried a number of medications, but the one that seemed to work the best was one I was allergic to. Dilantin kept the seizures to a minimum, but it also made me sleep and a lot of times it gave me welts on my skin and tongue. My mom kept taking me to different doctors, and we went through a series of tests, but we ended up at a dead end. The main doctor that treated me had told my mom that this was the best it was going to get. When he told her the real risk is of death from suffocation due to the oral swelling but that he had given up and wasn't going to try any other medication, my mom decided it was time to go back to L.A. We knew a very good doctor there who wasn't going to give up or limit treatment even if we didn't have any money.

So, again, we packed up only the things we really needed, saying good-bye to everything non-essential, and headed out to the next place.

Part Four:
Questionable Alternatives

He's back in the room tonight.
I don't how he got in.
But now the door is shut behind him.

Drop down.
He's big, he can't drop low so quickly.

The room is dark, no windows or furniture.
There's some light, but
where is it coming from?

It's the door behind him,
it looks shut but it's not.

He's standing above me.
He's huge, his hands scare me.
Now… He's going to hurt me now.

But not with his fists.
Watch his hands.
I think he's going to choke me.

I have to get to the door…

Court

Back in Los Angeles. Back to the drunks and bums of downtown. It was always a little scary downtown anywhere east of Spring, but still, L.A. is home and somehow I was hoping that being back home meant we could find some connection again. I felt like I had almost completely lost my mom somewhere in the mess of things, and I didn't know how I was going to live without her loving me. So, again, it was time to start anew.

When we first got back in town, of course we had very little money, so we had to figure out what we were going to do. We spent a little time staying at cheap hotels and going to churches to try to get some help. Most churches turned us away, but there was sometimes a handout or referral to somewhere or someone who could help.

I don't really know what my mom's plan was. We needed to figure out a long-term place to live, but we also needed to get medical attention. We did find Dr. Bell's office but learned that Dr. Bell, Sr. was retired; his son had taken over the medical office. Still, Mom's decision to get us back to L.A. for my medical attention proved to be a good one. Dr. Bell, Jr. did quickly get me off of Dilantin and on to a different medication that seemed to help. He also wanted to look at the seizures differently and sent me to a psychiatrist.

I had only one or two psych visits, but I got as much as possible from them. I don't remember the doctor's name but remember more his tone. I was really nervous, hoping I wouldn't say anything to get anyone in trouble. He was good at putting me at ease and just asked me a few questions. I remember him asking me about how the seizures felt, if I saw anything or smelled anything that told me a seizure was coming. I was in his office really trying to think of how I could answer him. There was something that would happen: A kind of uneasy feeling in my chest would come up to my throat, and then something would happen to the things around me; they would disappear. I just didn't know how to explain it and didn't want to seem like I wasn't trying. His voice was calming and he told me to just think about it, and when it was clear I might be able to say it. I didn't see him again after that appointment, but I kept his voice and his directions in my head. It felt good that he talked to me as though I actually had some insight into my own condition and that I just didn't know how to explain it yet. I worked on it for years before the seizures finally stopped in my late teens. For now, I would just keep trying to pay attention and be happy that someone suggested that I could figure things out.

While we were dealing with my medical problems, we had reconnected with a couple of Mom's old friends on Court Street, across from the corner market. The apartment was around the corner from where we had lived when I was an infant, and the couple we reconnected with was the same couple we had known at the Bon Aire Apartments. Silvia was the woman Mom had been arguing with when the car hit us. I wasn't sure if I should feel good that friendships could last longer than I had experienced or if this was proof that we would never get away from the same kinds of problems we kept having.

***

Roman and I sat quietly at the dining room table while Mom and Silvia talked in the kitchen. Silvia's husband, Carlos, was still at work, and her daughter, Leticia, was still in school. The house was clean and in some ways seemed well kept, but there was so much that just seemed wrong. I didn't know if it was because of everything we had been through or some other secrets in their home.

When Leticia got home and quickly walked through the room, both Roman and I reacted with surprise. This was the same person we knew as a young child five or so years ago? That seemed impossible. Leticia was full of rage in her every movement. I think it was because we were there that she went straight to her room. It seemed that the typical day would have seen an immediate fight as soon as she got home. Carlos arrived a short time later and joined Mom and Silvia in the kitchen for a little while before he went out to work on the car.

Silvia and Carlos first met at the Bon Aire Apartments through my mom when she was managing the units. They had been in a relationship for as long as I knew them, but it was far from a smooth connection. The household was full of anger with lots of drinking and fighting, exactly how things had been when we were all together before. We ended up staying at the Cruz home for a little while before moving into the place a block down.

While we were there, we saw why things felt so wrong . . . because they were. There were so many fights. Almost daily there was intense drinking and arguments that often turned violent. Carlos and Leticia would get into physical fights, and Carlos would shove Leticia across the room and knock her down to the floor. I never understood why things got so bad and why Carlos felt he had to beat up a kid, but the bigger question was why Silvia just sat there . . . just sat at the table complaining about wanting another drink. I remember one night Carlos had Leticia against the wall with his hand around her neck, and Silvia just walked into the kitchen, got a beer, and walked back out.

As I watched everything that was going on, I was telling myself to pay attention. I'd have to start learning how to take a hit and get out of a fight. I'd seen Mom get hurt in the past, but it had not involved me yet. When it does, I can't count on Mom to do anything to help, so I need to pay attention and figure out how I'm going to handle it when it starts.

The other thing I noticed was that no one came to visit the Cruz house. Other than the three of them, Leticia had a boyfriend who came by a couple times before she said good-bye to him, and Silvia's brother,

Hector, would come by now and then. Other than that, they seemed to have no friends they spent any time with. It seemed strange to me, but something about it made perfect sense. No friends visiting helped to manage containment. If things are this bad all the time, it's best not to go public by sharing too much with anyone outside the immediate family.

Hector

While we stayed at the Cruz house, I slept in the same bed as Leticia. Besides all the anger and fighting, I could tell something was wrong with her. I knew with her, just as with all the guys I had known, something was going to happen and she would approach me. It didn't really even occur to me to second-guess my instinct because she wasn't a man. The strange sense I felt around her was the same, so it was really just a matter of being ready when she made a move.

It didn't take long. Leticia started with me just after the first couple of nights—and was much bolder in her direct sexual moves than anything I had experienced before. She was in her mid-teens and had been sexually active for several years by then. I didn't know exactly what to do, because she seemed clear on her decision, but at the same time it felt like she was determined to get me to go along for some hidden reason. It was a little scary because of how forceful she was, but at least she was a girl. Somehow that leveled things out a little. I felt like I could predict more or at least that she couldn't say anything about her body that I wouldn't understand in my own.

She told me to just go along with things, and then nobody would get in trouble. I really didn't know what she meant, but I did get that there was always some kind of trouble. I went along but told her not to kiss me or touch my face. I would deal with anything else. The first night was mostly touching. Then as the weeks went on, the sexual acts became more frequent and more explicit. I was telling myself to go along just because I didn't feel physically threatened; I didn't imagine she would directly hit me. But I started objecting more as things continued and finally said I just didn't understand why this had to keep happening when I didn't want it to. Then Leticia said she wasn't doing it for pleasure. She told me that Hector was making her do it.

Hector? He's not even here when we have sex. Leticia told me that Hector had been having sex with her since she was eight and that he would make her do things with a lot of girls. She shared details about how mean Hector was and how violent sex with him was. I didn't really know what to do or what to think, but after remembering some of the men I knew, it wasn't hard to believe everything she was saying.

I kept going along, and things were getting more and more distorted. The things that Leticia wanted me to do moved from sex with her to taking nude photos for Hector and his friends, watching porn, and even going up to strangers and inviting sexual acts. I had been exposed to a lot of sexuality before this, but still, I was maybe ten years old and trying to figure out how far I had to go before I could get out.

I was disgusted by so much of what was happening and couldn't figure out Leticia's real angle. Was all this really because of Hector? I remember asking her when she introduced me to porn and I nearly threw up . . . *How would Hector know if I watched or not?* She told me as she had before that he keeps checking with her to see how far things had gone, but she didn't make me keep watching that night. She told me we would start slowly, and she would show me more movies later. It wasn't really new for me to have to keep up with all kinds of awful games, but I didn't understand why they just kept going. I had to figure out how to make things stop, because they were getting too crazy.

One of the things I learned with some of the guys before was that there was a benefit to having developed so early. I could use the fact that I had already started my period to have some influence over the things that would happen. In this case it wouldn't do anything to limit sex with Leticia, but I hoped it would end some of the solicitation games. It didn't.

Leticia told me that Hector wanted me to approach another man and have sex with him. It wasn't the first time he had wanted me to do this, but it was the first time he said he wanted proof; he wanted to see me pregnant. *What?* I didn't know how to even process that thought. I told Leticia I wouldn't do it. Leticia begged me to go along and told me that Hector was not going to take no for an answer. He would come to me himself or maybe to Roman. *Wait! This again? Is this possible?* I couldn't take a chance and just said that yes, I'd do it.

It was a drunk in the alley that was chosen for me to approach, and I did what I was told. I tried to think of ways I might be able to get away. I knew I couldn't leave, because where would I go? No one hires kids to do jobs that could sustain a life, and I didn't have any faith that my mom would do anything about things, so I had to get through it . . . but there was no way I could let myself become pregnant.

I went up to the man, tried to smile, and started directly in by unzipping his pants. I started to cry but kept going and hoped he would pass out or realize a crying child had approached him. Instead, he said his apartment was a block away and we could go there; we did. My crying didn't make him stop. He didn't speak much English, but he did hear me say that I had already had my period and that I didn't want to get pregnant. I pushed him off of me, and he finished by himself. I ran out of the apartment and had a rush of terrible thoughts. Things had gone too far and gotten too close to a possible pregnancy. If I get pregnant and bring a baby into this, then I am the same as all these other monsters. I can't do that—no matter what the punishment. I thought of Roman and told him in my mind that I was sorry, but I couldn't do it. I would do anything else to protect him, but I couldn't get pregnant.

I went back to the house and into the shed in the backyard where Leticia was waiting for a detailed report. I came back crying and angry. I told her I didn't let him get me pregnant and that there was no way I was going to go along with any more of Hector's rules. I wasn't even convinced that Hector was really in control. I told Leticia that she couldn't threaten me anymore. If Hector wanted something, he would have to show up and tell me himself.

I was scared, because I really didn't know how much control Hector had. If he really was behind everything, then he must have Leticia completely terrified, which meant he was more cruel than I wanted to believe. If he's not the one in control, then Leticia was the cruel one. Either way, I had to do something. I felt like I had already lost myself, and I was afraid that my mistakes would soon come to the point I was most afraid of . . . they would cost me my brother either through his direct harm or with him seeing me as the problem.

A couple days later, Hector finally showed up to talk with me face to face. There was a back room, like a covered porch, where he called me in from the yard. I was scared just looking at him. He was big and mean-hearted. He stood there holding a rat while he talked to me. He told me that he heard I wasn't doing what I was told and that I wanted to see him. I was filled with fear and a rush of thoughts. I suddenly remembered Leonard and reminded myself that I knew what I was looking at. Hector was dangerous just like Leonard was, even though their ways were different. Hector seemed meaner and more directly threatening. For a moment I remember feeling like Leonard was just practice. With Hector, I had to be tougher and stand taller, because he really liked what he was doing and had no interest in me or my family. At least Leonard had a legal connection through marriage. Hector could easily just disappear, and no one would even ask about him.

I thought fast and told myself to speak as few words as possible; I can't let him hear my voice tremble. "I didn't want to do what I was told." I spoke as clearly as I could and felt like I was yelling, but my actual voice still sounded very small. I told myself not to let my own weak sound show up in my face: *Do not bow down. Keep looking up.*

Hector responded by squeezing the rat in his hand, making it squeal out in pain. I knew he was trying to scare me and I needed to just stand my ground and not cry or run. I saw the rat and saw his hand but reminded myself not to be distracted from looking directly at Hector's face. I had made that mistake before; I won't do it again.

Hector talked about how Leticia and the other girls really liked the things he had them do and always came back for more. I kept still, standing and listening, trying to figure out my next move. Hector helped with that when he went on to tell me that it would be either me or my brother, but one of us was going to say yes.

Yes, he is just like Leonard. It's good that I didn't bow down; I can't just go along. That didn't work last time. Now what? Remember Jack's brother . . . "I could just tell them what you're doing." I looked straight at him when I said it. It was only partly a bluff. I thought of all the other things I had tried in the past and none of them worked, but there was something about the secrecy . . . even when people know what's going on, nobody does anything. But as soon as it's announced—actually stated out loud for others to hear—there's a problem with continuing. I didn't really know if my mom would care, but now there are other people involved so maybe someone would. If he called my bluff, I was willing to scream loudly that moment. What do I have to lose?

"You won't say anything." His face told me that he was actually not sure if I would or not. Hector, I later learned, did in fact abuse a lot of girls. He knew how to choose them and how to approach them. I think he also knew that I was not new to abuse. I think that gave him a suggestion that I maybe would do something to try to get away from him.

"How do you know I won't?" I asked him based on what I thought I heard in his voice and saw on his face. I wasn't sure what he would do, and I was a little scared that even if he left me and Roman alone, he would punish Leticia. But I couldn't back down or show my worries right now. I just have to get past this confrontation.

Hector didn't respond to my question but instead laughed at me, threw the rat down, and went into the house. I didn't tell anyone about the discussion and tried to tell myself I would be ready to deal with his punishment if it came. I came up with plans for how I would scream and break things to get the neighbors' attention and looked at every window and doorway in the house in case I needed to break out. I decided that this time I would at least make a loud ugly mess to call him out in front of everyone. Even if it didn't end the whole problem, I would at least have witnesses for one event.

After a couple weeks with no word from him and no other instructions or threats through Leticia, I saw that my bluff had worked. I would occasionally still see him, with the group of young girls he had already trained to do what he wanted, in a car driving by and waving to me. But outside of that, I did not see Hector face to face after the back porch discussion and his requests through Leticia stopped.

Downtown

A lot of things went on while we were on Court Street. Mom was dating and drinking a lot. We were again living in a single apartment, though by now Roman and I needed some privacy; I was ten, and he was eleven. So everyone got their own designated space. Roman's bedroom was a small sectioned off part of the kitchen that was marked by a curtain and mine was the closet next to the bathroom. Mom had her bed in the main room, also sectioned off with a curtain.

Even though we found our own place, since the Cruz house was so close and Mom didn't really have any other friends, we would go back and forth between the two places a lot. Mom's drinking would get really bad, and then she'd ease up for a bit. But she really didn't stop for more than a couple days at a time. There was a local bar just a few blocks away that she would spend time at to find dates. I was always mixed in my feelings when she went out. I was relieved that I wouldn't have to deal with her drinking at home but always worried that she would get hurt, or worse, that she'd bring the guy home and he'd do his damage here. I remember one night Mom came home looking worse than usual. She was slobbering drunk and talking a lot. I was always angry when she came home drunk, but this time something more serious was wrong.

I was so angry with my mom about everything and in a real way felt that there was already so much lost that I really wanted to just turn away and cut her out of my life. But that was impossible; she was still Mom, and right now she needed someone. She was walking up the stairs to our apartment, leaning on the banister as she went. I looked closer and saw blood on her face and her blouse was open. She said she was raped at the bar.

I didn't know what to do and never knew how she was going to act when she was drunk. I asked her if the guy was gone and if I should call the police. "No police!" She just needed coffee and a shower but also wanted to tell me what had happened. She kept talking in the hallway, and I started to cry. I told her I didn't know what to do when she tells me that someone had raped her but I can't call the police. And now she wants me to listen to what happened. She started to get mad and raised her voice, telling me that she needed some help. I always felt so guilty when she wanted me to talk to her about things I could do nothing about. I would try to find my own voice and tell myself that I was not the mother; I wasn't the one who was supposed to fix everything, but just like tonight, there was always a crisis and I didn't know how to just walk away when she was so scared.

I helped her into the apartment and cleaned her up. I listened to her talk about the man who had raped her. She said he was new to the bar and that he wouldn't be coming back; he would just move on. I hated hearing some of the details about how he pinned her down and hit her even though she said she wouldn't fight. But as she was talking, I started listening in a way to help me figure out how to handle a rape when it happens to me. I asked her how she knew it was rape. Guys she had sex with had hit her before. How was this one different?

She started explaining that most men would eventually hit a woman and a lot of them hurt women during sex, but that is not rape. Rape is when the man forces a woman to have sex. I paid close attention to the definition and tried to figure out what my experiences were and tried to compare some of the recent ones with what she was describing. Was I *forced*? Or maybe the question is, was it really sex? I didn't know.

A couple months after Hector disappeared, Luis, Silvia's son, showed up and started approaching me almost immediately. I didn't understand a lot of what he did, but the way he handled things was very familiar. He was all about mind games. He'd try to convince me that he knew people in my past and that he had talked with my mom and she wanted us to be together. I didn't believe him but felt like I knew this game, and even if he hadn't talked with my mom, she would end up saying yes to anything when he did. I felt I was on my own and had to decide how to deal with him.

It was one day when I was at the Cruz house when somehow I ended up in the basement with Luis. I'm still confused when I think about it, but certain parts are still so clear. I was watching and knew something was going to happen, but this was new. Not completely new, exactly, but . . . I can't really explain it except to say that I knew something was going to happen and that I'd have to be tough enough to take it. The basement was unfinished, and I was sitting on the floor where there was this incline. That part of the ground was either completely uncovered or maybe had busted cement. Luis looked at me with some kind of deliberate intent. He said he was sorry he had to be the one to do this to me and then quickly pushed me to my back, dropped down on his knees, and raised his fist, ready to punch me. The second I knew what was going to happen, I spoke out. "Don't hit my face—it'll bruise!"

No, I didn't tell him to not hit me or beg him to let me go. What was the point of that? I knew this would happen eventually, and I think he was being easier on me than someone else would. He said he was sorry and let me know what was going to happen. I won't always get a warning. I just have to get the rules down, and one thing I've learned is that no one is supposed to know. So no face bruises.

I spoke fast enough that he heard. He quickly made eye contact before he swung his fist down to punch my breast. It knocked the breath out of me, and I felt myself starting to cry. I tried to keep my eyes open and look at him, but it was too hard to take the hits and keep myself focused. I closed my eyes and told myself the beatings never took long . . . *just a few hits, and it will be over. Maybe just a minute. Just a few more, and it's over.* I tried a couple times to look at him again simply to learn how to tell when the rage was gone. He stuck to the agreement and only hit me below the neck.

When it was done, I looked at him to see what this was really about. I remembered Jack and looked for the same connection with Luis. There was something there, but it wasn't the same. Jack seemed like he was really trying to figure something out. For Luis, it seemed that this was nothing new for him. I almost felt it was a practice run to see how I would react. He watched me, waiting to see what I would do and then told me I could tell anyone I wanted, but no one was going to do anything. I knew he was right, so I didn't bother saying anything, and we went on as usual, except now I was looking for a sign of the next incident.

Going on meant that incidents continued with Luis and soon went from violent to sexual. And as I expected, the next physical attack was different; the practice round had passed. The next few attacks were less controlled and more directly driven by rage. I learned that my role was to be available and ready when he needed to physically release his anger. I also learned that what I was worried about was real . . . there was something that got confused with the violence and sexual acts. Luis started mixing the two in a way I hadn't dealt with before. The first time he was sexual after hitting me, he used an object to penetrate me; I don't even know what it was. After he was done, I was crying and bleeding, but the part that was so confusing was the fact that he acted as if it was supposed to be something good. He started talking about how much he loved me and how important I was to him.

I thought about this incident while I listened to my mom talk about rape. I may not have asked for it, but was I really forced? No, I could have done something. Plus, Luis wasn't a stranger. It wasn't normal sex, and he spoke kindly to me afterward. So, no, I guess it wasn't rape. I guess it was just the regular stuff she talked about when she said men often hurt women during sex.

***

I eventually learned that Mom knew about things that were happening. She knew Luis was hitting me and knew that there were events with other men in the neighborhood. It seemed that this time there was no pretending to be uninformed anymore. Instead, knowing what was going on almost seemed to make my mom like me more . . . or she at least seemed to give me more advice that she meant as helpful. I was sad that somehow my becoming the same kind of person she was seemed to be the only thing that made my mom want to help me. Is this what she really wanted for me? For me to just take it and become one more woman that gets hit and is afraid of men? I actually think that is what she wants. It seemed to please her that we would have things to talk about now, and she could tell me secrets and give special insights about how to be better at taking stuff. It was so complicated in my head. I still needed my mom and now there's something that made her want to be close to me. We started doing more things together . . . listening to music more, playing cards, and talking more about life overall. I held on tight to the moments I could be close to her but still kept wondering how far along she expected me to keep going and if there would be a time when she would start helping me imagine a different kind of life.

I got my answer to that question one day when I was sitting at the top of the stairs in the hallway outside the apartment. "You know, honey, you're growing up." My mom started talking to me in what sounded like an effort to be comforting. "A lot of girls don't have their family to support them, but I want you to know that if you get pregnant, it's okay. We'll get you on food stamps and welfare, and we'll keep the baby."

I heard her offer in a voice that said she really thought this was an important and special gift she was giving me. Maybe it was, and I was just too young or too arrogant to hear it. Instead, what I heard was something that left me almost speechless and genuinely disappointed. She really doesn't have any expectations of me or my life getting any better. I am only ten years old—what about school or work or anything else? I knew that she really meant what she had said years ago: The best I will get is a guy who will hit me.

I felt even more alone and abandoned. How did I lose my mom when she has been right here living with me all this time? And how is it that she is working to reconnect now that she believes my future is so dark? What, exactly, do I say to her offer? Nothing. I said nothing. I swallowed my sadness and realized that Mom will never have any vision of a future for me unless I am sitting next to her talking about how to get my check cashed and how to cook the right dinner so I don't get hit that night.

***

I kept going along and trying to figure out my place in everything. I knew I wouldn't have a place in the house as her daughter much longer if I didn't learn to go along and make things work with Luis. But I also knew I didn't want a lifetime of figuring out how to maneuver around angry outbursts. So, again, I told myself to pay attention and try to see something Mom doesn't.

The day came soon enough when I tried to connect differently with Luis when he hit me. I don't recall why he was mad that day, but we were at the apartment by ourselves and I saw he was going to hit me. I can't exactly explain it, but we had developed our own communication and pattern with the physical abuse. This time, I tried to look more closely at him to see what was going on. Somehow I knew that the hits were not because I'd done something, even though

Mom talked as though women did something to make them happen. I knew Luis was just angry, and I had a deep sense of my own anger that I had promised myself I would never inflict on anyone else. I wasn't good at choosing my words, but I attempted to say I knew he had too much anger to talk about and that was why he hit me and destroyed things around him. It didn't keep Luis from continuing with his outburst, but it did give me a different mental position. I started thinking about how much anger there was in life and accepted that there had to be some people who acted on it before they learned to do something else. I figured Luis was one of the many that still had to learn another way . . . and I hadn't yet learned that I could expect something else. Until I did, somehow I knew the abuse would keep going. In a very confusing way, I took the mental position of seeing my own anger being taken out on me through another person's rage, though I didn't even begin to fully identify this mental position until many years later.

***

While I was trying to figure out how or if there was any way I could talk to Luis about his anger and keep myself from getting hit, the rest of life kept going on. I was still in school, but it seemed like such a joke. I was in fifth grade, and the school was just four blocks away, but I would show up a few times and then miss a couple weeks. I would read enough to prove I could learn and would show up to take a math test, but other than that, my priorities were more about home. Of course, I didn't say that when the principal talked to me and told me that I needed to come to school more. I would just work the timing to try to keep him from calling my mom too often. When it finally got to be too much, I did have to show up with my mom in his office.

I argued that I wasn't learning anything in class, so there was no point in showing up when there were things I could be doing at home. The principal grew tired of me quickly and said if that was true I should be tested to prove I was above my assigned level. Luckily I did well on the test, so my argument was taken as a valid reason for my absence. I was moved up to the next grade, which meant if I could get through the next three months without being called in, then I would be able to leave the school and not deal with the principal again. My sixth-grade teacher liked me but also saw something was wrong and didn't give me a hard time when I missed class. So even with several more absences in the last three months, I passed my tests and finished the school year with no more visits to the principal.

At home, things were the same in general: lots of drinking and fighting. Mom kept going out and finding guys. Most were left at the bar or would stay just one night at the apartment until Adam showed up. It was clear the first time Mom introduced him that he wasn't going to be a short-timer. I tried to like Adam just because I knew he wasn't going anywhere. We were about due for a new live-in guy. Mom liked him, and he didn't make any move toward me, which was a relief. I watched how he was with my mom and was glad there was no expectation that he'd somehow become "Dad."

I remember feeling that any room I had in the home was disappearing. Mom had already started treating me like I was on my own in a lot of ways, which wasn't really new, but now she was less and less available. And I really believed she was ready to put her date ahead of her kids. I started trying to prepare myself for another change, but I wasn't quite sure what it would be.

Adam moved in with us for a while. I never knew the details of how they had met and why he moved in so quickly, but it happened even though there were problems that came up right from the beginning. Adam was handy and could be charming, but was really angry and would often get into arguments at work and lost jobs quickly. He also almost immediately started problems with the apartment management. He complained about the apartment and would make accusations about people following him and targeting him. He made trouble for us that my mom had to deal with to try to keep us from getting evicted. It didn't take long for his anger to show up violently with my mom.

He started hitting her during arguments just a few weeks into the relationship. I couldn't figure out exactly what all of his triggers were, but it seemed his jealously showed up a lot. Jealousy in such a strange way, though. My mom was not flirtatious and didn't compare her current man with any others, but she did have interests. Music was one of them. She loved Sammy Davis, Jr. and had a nice collection of his stuff. Music was one of the things Mom and I were able to connect on, and we would go to music stores and look up all of Sammy's records in the big yellow book that was up in front at the counter. We would search for the albums she hadn't yet found. Adam would make sarcastic remarks about how much Mom liked Sammy and how much she talked about our finding records. Then one day he didn't want to hear any more and lost his temper. He hit my mom and busted all her records. I told my mom we should make him leave; she shouldn't be afraid of collecting records or spending time with her daughter. But no, she would stay with Adam and just listen to Sammy on the old radio station.

I was so mad at my mom for letting this guy live with us without knowing anything about him and for continuing to let him stay even now that we know enough to see that he was a hitter. I couldn't understand how she just said it was okay. She would stay with him and let him be abusive. She saw that he would not only pick fights with her but would argue with anyone around. He'd pick on our home and complained in a way that put us at risk of losing our space. I watched closely and again made a promise to myself. I told myself that I'd never live with a guy who cost me my home . . . another promise I tried to keep but failed.

I started thinking of what would happen if he got us kicked out. Where would I go? I argued with my mom about it, but she told me that it was her time to be happy again so she would be with Adam and I could decide where I would be. It was just a few months later when we had to move. Adam told my mom that he knew a place where he could get a room for a cheap price downtown. They moved at the end of the month, and I was going back and forth between the Cruz house and downtown.

I started looking around for anything else. I looked older than I was, an eleven-year-old who could pass for fifteen. Or if I dressed and talked right, maybe sixteen. But I still wasn't old enough to get a real job, so I looked at other options. Churches could offer a few hours of quiet space but no real solution. Shelters usually meant somehow going into the system and risking my connection with my brother, so that left street prostitution or some other kind of sexual trade. I started looking around to see what kind of person I'd have to be with if I decided to find some random man to live with for a trade deal.

I thought I'd have to really be clever or put in a lot of time to find options, but as it turned out, I quickly discovered that there was no shortage of men who were more than willing to take in a lost girl as long as she was clear on the house rules and agreed to the specifics of the sexual trade. I would spend a few hours a day looking around and was truly surprised that there was not one day I didn't have several offers from different men. Somehow even with everything I'd seen, I had not developed a stomach for this kind of life. The men made me sick, and I couldn't go through with any offers that were made. I soon accepted that my only choices were to figure things out and make it work with Luis or break away and rejoin my mom and Adam.

At first I was really thinking that this was my time to just accept that I had to start living my life separated from my mom. She had Adam now, and she was actually encouraging me to make things work with Luis. So I spent some time at the Cruz house where Luis usually was so I could see if I could make things work. I did what I could to contribute to the house. I cooked and cleaned, and did what I could to help in the yard. I didn't make any statement that I was ready to start a life with Luis but did do what I could to try to understand his patterns to prepare myself if I wasn't welcomed to move with my mom and Adam. They had just moved into a room in a hotel on 2nd Street just off of San Pedro.

My relationship with Luis continued with a lot of the same patterns. We would get along okay for a few days then something would happen and some kind of strange sex and physical outburst would come. I tried not to lose myself and stuck with my thoughts of trying to become someone who could learn to be a good wife and help her man know he didn't have to turn to hitting when he was mad. I would talk to Luis about not wanting to stay if it meant he would keep hitting me.

We went through some incidents when he didn't hit me, but then he started talking about suicide.

Talk of death didn't get the result I think he wanted. I did what people are told to do, which was try to talk him out of it, but when he kept going on about it, I told him that he couldn't blame me if he decided to kill himself.

On one of the days he started talking about how he would kill himself, I didn't show any sympathy but told him if he wanted to do it, he should just go ahead and do something but not drag me into it. He got mad at me and started yelling about how I was like everyone else and didn't care about anyone but myself. I was already unsure of whether I could make things work with him and the Cruz family; this new angle of blaming told me I would never be able to do anything here that wasn't about taking some form of punishment or blame. I told him I was leaving and started walking away to head downtown and see if I could still live with Mom.

I had tried to leave Luis before but was never successful. He would talk with my mom, and she would tell me that he was really a good person and that I should try to make it work. We even went through a period where I told my mom that I didn't want to be with Luis, and she told me that she was going to keep talking to him and when I was ready, she'd talk to both of us. During that short phase, Mom didn't talk to me when Luis was around. She would only talk to him. A mean punishment, I thought, but it worked. I was never good at taking the silent treatment from anyone, and it was horrible from my mom . . . to just be erased with no acknowledgment because she was making a point. I still think ignoring and intentional silence is a much harsher punishment than most people deserve.

When I left this time, Luis followed me and changed his tone to something immediately softer and more charming. He ran after me and called for me to come back; I kept walking. When he finally caught up with me and tried to get me to change my mind, he pointed out all the things he had done for me, trying to prove I was important to him. He was trying to learn not to be so angry. He pointed out that he had run after me and fell on the way, that he was willing to look like a fool and do whatever I wanted. I didn't respond except to say that I was leaving, and he wouldn't be able to live with me. The truth is that he was living off his family, and if he thought he could live off of my mom, I think he would have just followed along. But since Adam was there, he knew another man wouldn't pay his way, so he stopped following me.

I kept walking down through the 2nd Street tunnel before I turned around again to make sure he wasn't there. Nothing—I was finally rid of him and felt like this could be my first move toward a different life. I knew I'd have to live with Mom, but I would know that I could get away from the kind of life she told me I would have. For now, though, I'd have to figure out how to get to her new place and have her let me stay without trying to push me back to Luis.

I showed up and talked to my mom, telling her I needed to be there with her. I told her that I had failed and didn't know how to make things work with Luis. I told her that Luis had started talking about suicide, and I didn't want to be a part of that decision. The things I told her were not untrue, but I had to say everything in a way that made me the failure. If I said things the way I felt, I would have said that I was finally strong enough to know that I had to leave Luis if I wanted to save myself. That, however, would have made her send me back, and I really needed a place to stay.

Part Five:
Taking My Place

Back in the old neighborhood.
I know these streets, I know the park,
the lake, the freeway. I know every step.

But where is everyone?
I don't think I am home – something
here is false – watch my back,
I must.

It's night, I am walking in the street,
but no cars are around.
Not driving by, not parked, nowhere.

The streetlights are on so I can see if
I am being followed.
I need to get home.

Someone is following me,
a man a couple blocks away.
He scares me.

Something else is wrong…
it is not a man.
Something is wrong here,

I'm not going to get away from it –
It will do more than hurt me.

I am in its territory; this is not my home.
I have to go.
(wake up)

It keeps getting closer – what is it?
(Wake Up)

I start to run; it follows, transforming into a lion.
(WAKE UP)

Under the freeway, it jumps me; it has pinned me
down on my back and is in my face.
(WAKE UP!)

He told me I shouldn't have come back; he would
never let me go.
(BOBBIE!   WAKE UP!!!)

The Hotel

The place Adam found was a single-room unit with a common bathroom in an old hotel on 2nd Street just off of San Pedro, a couple blocks from the homeless district. The hotel was a magnet for low-life tenants but still held itself in high regard since it offered maid service and rejected hourly rate customers. Roman and I stayed with Mom and Adam in the single room on the third floor for a couple months before we got a second room right next door.

For the first few weeks there seemed to be some attempt not so much to really make things work smoothly but an agreement that the violent outbursts would be kept between Mom and Adam and not in front of me and Roman. There was some pattern where my mom would iron Adam's clothes when he got up to go to or look for work. There'd be a few days where he would work, and then something would happen at work to piss him off. There would be a fight at home with both of them drinking way too much. Then Adam would just stop going to work, or he'd be too hung over to get up. Once he did get up, it would be either Mom doing what she was supposed to do not to upset him or if it was too late, he'd get up angry and the arguments would start immediately.

There were a few occasions when they held off until Roman and I were out, but the effort to go through their routine without involving me or Roman didn't last long. We soon got to repeated events of things escalating and either resulting in neighbors getting involved or Roman stepping in to try to keep Mom from getting hit. I've always hated my mom for that. I thought she should be embarrassed that she not only allowed her twelve-year-old son to take a hit for her but she started to look to him to intervene.

Like I did, I think Roman started looking around for his own options to find something other than the life we had at home. He would spend some time with us but started to spend more time at the home of friends he met at school. Over the years, Roman found a second family with them and spent a lot of time going back and forth between our place and theirs.

***

When we expanded our home at the hotel from one unit to two, Roman and I stayed in the unit we started out in while Mom and Adam moved into the housekeeping room next door. They had gotten into arguing almost daily and physically fighting several times a week. Police activity was nothing new at the hotel. Among the excessive drug use, shootings, and random dead bodies, our reports of domestic violence didn't seem at all out of place. We had gotten to the point where I had called so many times and Adam was arrested and released so many times that the police refused to come out unless it was "life-threatening." That meant that I couldn't call when I saw things were escalating, but instead I had to stay around and watch, then call for help when I could report details that would communicate an immediate emergency.

I had started sitting in the hallway on the floor outside of their room most evenings so I could hear things that were said and interrupt if I thought things would get physical. Random homeless visitors were nothing new at the hotel, so when I sat out there, I had several people come to me and ask if I needed a place to stay. Most were people I was happy to just answer and never speak to again, but one seemed more sincere in his question. David was a young Japanese guy that lived a couple doors down from us. He spoke broken English and seemed to want to keep a respectful distance to not intrude but also seemed to want to offer some comfort to a girl who clearly needed it.

Even though he was really a stranger, David did a lot to help me. He would watch out for me and do little things like walk with me to the corner store when it was late and check in to let me know if he was going to be out so I could watch TV in his room if I wanted to get away from a fight. I remember one day when I walked out of the building onto 2nd Street, David was standing out there with some of the other tenants. Mom and Adam were screaming and fighting so loud that they could be heard on the street. It was embarrassing, and there was no way I could pretend I wasn't involved. The hotel was full of violent drug abusers and had its share of guests with mental illnesses, but we were the only family with kids who lived there and had a constant stream of problems that seemed we were all too willing to make public. It didn't matter that I was surrounded by people who would be considered socially unacceptable in some way, I was the one who was really ashamed of my life and didn't want to face anyone, so I kept my head down.

When I walked out with the others already there, all talk came to a halt. In a strange way, it seemed that no matter how many problems everyone there had, there was still a recognition that I was a kid dealing with all the problems of a violent home, and there were no magic words that could fix it. I could feel the weight of the silence with no one knowing what to say or how to even address me. David broke the tension with a smile and a gesture, waving his hand up toward my mom's voice as though to tell me to throw all that away. I looked at him and tried to offer a smile of acknowledgment but nearly broke down crying; the best I could do was stand silently. After another moment of awkwardness, David put on an exaggerated expression of excitement and tried to say something in his broken English as if to say he had found "the answer."

I had no idea what he was talking about but did recognize that he was trying to offer something to make me feel better. I gave an expression of gratitude—mixed, I'm sure, with some confusion—just before he made another gesture suggesting I wait for him. He walked away down the street toward San Pedro. I wasn't really sure what to do, but he had indicated that

I should not leave so I decided to stand there a few minutes. I probably need a little time to collect my thoughts and keep my head together anyway.

So I stood there, and sure enough, just a few minutes later, I saw David coming back with a brown paper bag in his hand. I felt myself start to lighten up as I saw him coming closer with a kind of silly energy in his walk. When he got close enough, he presented the bag to me like he had discovered gold. I started cautiously smiling. He then reached into the bag and pulled out two ice cream treats, one ice cream sandwich and one Eskimo Pie. I took the Eskimo Pie. He took the ice cream sandwich and stepped back to lean on the parking meter where he was standing before and started unwrapping his ice cream. I heard what he was telling me and quietly agreed that it was better to be out here eating ice cream with a friend than to get lost listening to a fight that I had nothing to do with. I didn't know it at the time, but David ended up being a real friend to me over the next couple years.

***

Mom and Adam continued their routine with the drinking and fights. I went to school sometimes, often not. I was really at a point where school was simply not a priority. I still think of that time and want to roll my eyes at the choice in front of me: go learn a new math trick or stay at home and do what I can to keep my mom from getting killed? I chose the latter. I stayed close to home and often got a few hours of housekeeping or laundry work. I kept my eyes and ears open to be prepared to step in or call for help when things got bad. Roman would put himself between Mom and Adam when he was there; when he wasn't, David often showed up to shield my mom. It wasn't long, maybe a few months, before things escalated to a point where the fight got bad enough for the police to show up again.

Who knows what started it, but it was an evening when Adam hit my mom in the head with something and she went down hard. Police and paramedics showed up that night. Normally, if either showed up, I was the one to talk with them and try to get some option for doing something. But the bottom line was that if my mom refused to press charges, Adam would not be arrested unless the injuries were life-threatening. *So he has to kill her first?* I wanted things to be different, but I knew there was nothing I could do; she would have to decide to have him arrested. Mom finally agreed and that night said yes, she would press charges.

Adam was taken away, and Mom was told what to do to get a restraining order to keep him away. We were surprised that he was released so quickly that time. He showed up early the next morning, knocking at the door. I was with my mom in the room and told her not to let him in. She could not claim to "forgive" and then start everything over again—not if she was true about wanting to take care of her kids.

My mom was overwhelmed, crying, and panicked. Adam was talking softly outside the door, telling her how important she was and listing things he did to prove he was trying to do things the right way. He went on about how hard his life had been and how he had done everything he could for my mom. I listened and watched my mom struggle. She softened her voice and answered him with words like "I know how hard you've tried" and "I know you love me." With every word of comfort she spoke, I grew more fearful and angry.

"You can't open that door," I told her in a hard, cold tone that left no room for sympathy or excuse. I told her that he was not honest and to wait and see how he would change when he didn't get his way. She looked at me with a sense of begging permission to unlock the door. Again, I told her not to do it. I went as far as telling her now was the time to make a decision . . . "open the door and lose your kids because there is no way you can ask us to be in this with you." I knew I was taking a risk by speaking for both me and Roman, but my thought was that if she chose Adam after seeing how much he had hurt us and after how she had forced her son to fight her fights for her, then she should lose us.

In a way, Adam helped her make the decision. She did start to open the door, but before he got back in the room, Adam did change and started immediately calling names and tried to fight his way in. We pushed hard against the door and slammed it shut before he made it. I looked at my mom with so much anger and asked her again, "Which do you want?" She agreed that she would not let Adam in again and admitted that she would need help to keep him out. I hated that I was the one she wanted to help her but I was glad that at least the decision had been made that Adam would not continue to have a place in our lives.

Old Enough

True to form, even without Adam, my mom continued drinking and seemed to very quickly find a lot of friends to stay drunk with. She also, however, knew there was no one to help us financially, so she talked to the hotel owner about a job. She started with odd handyman-type work that she had done for many years. It came as no surprise when she was first turned down. She had been reminded for many years that this kind of work was not for women and knew it would be about proving herself up front and not about what she might say.

She told the owner that he could name anything that his current worker was doing or couldn't figure out how to do, and she would take care of it. She ended up getting hired on after she did some quick plumbing on a tub that the current worker had failed at fixing after several attempts. Mom was never worried about her ability to prove her work, and in this case, she again got what she needed. We would hear a few more times from Adam, but soon our last conversation with him was a call letting us know he would be doing some time so we wouldn't be seeing him. My mom wasn't up to taking the call, but I was glad to and took the time to let him know he wouldn't be missed.

With Adam gone and my own success with leaving Luis, I had moments of feeling hopeful that my mom and I could figure out how to be okay together without having to find another violent guy. We never exactly were successful though. I spent most of the time in an almost autopilot state. It was as though I was numb, just going through the motions most of the time with moments of rage and panic, wondering what my life would turn into.

Mom built up a regular job doing maid service and handyman work at the hotel. I also did maid service and some desk work. With her now working several days at the hotel, we were able to move to the fourth floor, into one of the much sought-after home apartment suites with the common bathroom a few doors down the hall and eventually had enough to rent the single room next door.

Life returned to much of what seemed familiar with continued drinking, poker nights, strange people around and Mom finding a lot of dates. I was glad we had a separate room so when she had her dates I could be completely out of the picture when the guy was there for the night. It helped to a degree, but since the guys she dated were also in the general social group that would come by to drink and play cards, I was still in the way when they visited. And the mix of people we were with seemed so careless to me. There were already too many years of questionable things happening but it seemed we were now moving deeper into some dark space than I had expected or knew how to manage.

We were around a lot of drug users and openly sexual people. Before this we had been around drug users but none so open or so messed up. I saw people in such low and desperate ways that it was terrifying to watch. I had also already seen and been in the middle of a lot of sexual situations but again never so publicly blatant with prostitution performed in the alleys or hallways, and my mom's boyfriends openly inviting me to have sex with them in front of her. I remember one specific guy, Jerry. He was short, well built, and acted as though he thought himself very attractive. My mom agreed and was with him for a couple months. I never liked Jerry; I thought he was creepy and never took him seriously as a person. I never got why my mom liked him, but I figured he was her choice and her problem. But then, once they were finished dating, Jerry approached me and asked if I was sexually interested. I wasn't surprised that he made the offer, but it did seem extra offensive in how he did it.

I was standing at the ironing board working through a load of shirts. My mom was there drinking with one a couple of neighbors and saw when Jerry leaned over the end of the board to get a little closer as he talked to me. He told me that everything with my mom was done so now we could have some fun. I was trying to figure out how anyone could be interested in this guy and felt disgusted that he would even attempt to approach me. I looked in my mom's direction and heard one of the neighbors tell her to watch out, because Jerry was hitting on me. I was glad that someone had pointed this out, even if only to suggest that Mom's thirty-something-year-old ex-boyfriend was being inappropriate by asking her thirteen-year-old daughter if she was sexually interested in him. My mom's response was that I was always more mature than my age and that it is something she has had to learn to accept. She knows that I am old enough to make the decision myself, and she wasn't going to get in the way; she and Jerry were finished. I brushed off Jerry's attempt to invite me but listened to my mom's words and got a mental reminder that I would have to quickly be prepared to take care of myself even though I knew I wasn't ready yet.

***

I was still looking around to figure out why life seemed to be such the cycle it was, but tried to tell myself that I would need to find a way to make a living and support my own life. That would be key: *Do something so you can have your own home and not be afraid living in someone else's.* I know that leaving Luis was an important thing to do, but I'm not ready yet to be on my own completely. So I have to hurry up and figure things out.

I kept working for the hotel and found other odd jobs as I could. I made calls for people, ran errands, cleaned window blinds for an old Japanese man who had stacks and stacks of newspapers and strange items like empty match boxes and paper towel rolls. Most of the money I earned would go toward the house, but the main thing was that I wanted to learn as much as I could about finding work anywhere so I would know how to support myself as an adult.

I also kept trying to understand the whole cycle of things that kept happening. I started talking to people, men mostly, about why it is so common for women to get hit. Most people didn't have much to say about it but stuck with general statements about how it depends on what the woman did. I never argued but kept asking for more information. Marcus was one of the guys that hung out at our place and the only one that would keep talking in more detail about why women get hit. He started telling me that it is not exactly the woman's fault but it come from how she thinks she's doing something right but does it for a man who has low tolerance. An example he gave was when I offered to wash his shirt.

"Just like that, you see? You are trying to do something nice, but if you did this for your husband one night and didn't do it again, then he might hit you." I followed his explanation but then asked why would anyone ever do anything caring if it meant there would be a punishment for it? I offered to wash his shirt because that's part of what I was taught. If the guys are working, then the women do things like wash and iron laundry. Marcus was the only guy in the mix that was working at the time, and he brought food to the house, so why wouldn't I give some offering to show I appreciated his contribution?

We continued the discussion, and he told me that not all women show their appreciation and that if I was going to be that kind of woman, I would have to make it clear that it is an offering and that the man should not expect it to be repeated. Again, I got the point he was making, but I asked him where the man was supposed to be responsible. I used myself as the example. "I am washing your shirt today, because I want to thank you for helping us with groceries. So tomorrow, if you bring more groceries and I don't wash your shirt, will you want to hit me?"

He laughed a little and said no, he wouldn't, but I can't look at this with the idea that I would be able to get around getting hit. I would have to be clear that the man I am with should not expect help from me and when I gave him any I would have to be sure to tell him not to expect more. I told him I was glad to talk about it, but I don't believe that ALL men resort to hitting their women when they don't get what they want. He agreed that it may not be all men, but most. I liked talking to Marcus—not so much because I agreed or disagreed with him, but because he did actually engage in the discussion and pose his own questions on whatever topic. It was partially because of that that I continued washing out his shirt after work until he got another one to alternate wearing.

***

I'm not sure what happened, but there was a strange time when we had some different people around. *Different* meaning not our regular friends, but still personalities that fit in with our regular selection of acquaintances. My mom was going through something and seemed to go up and down with her anger. I was going through major depressive swings. I had started again looking for more options to get out. I knew getting a real job would take some time just because of my age. I'd need to feel my way through at least another five years before I would even begin to be considered for a legal full-time job. School was still more of a nuisance than anything. We were getting lots of visits from social workers since my school attendance had decreased to near total dropout level. I was reminded through those visits that there are some things that are just too much for anyone to really deal with. I remember one day when the social worker showed up after who knows how many weeks of absences I had. I opened the door when he arrived, and he told me that I needed to go back to school.

I walked back over to the ironing board and let him see everything going on. My mom wasn't there, there were beer cans and liquor bottles all over the place, everything was a mess and I was standing there ironing clothes. I told him I wouldn't be going back. I remember his face when he heard my reply. It was an expression of not knowing where to even start. "I know," I said. "Take a look around." I don't think he knew what to say about what was in front of him but just said he would be back the next day if I wasn't in school. "Okay, I'll see you tomorrow."

He came back a couple of times before I think he told the school there was no use of his visiting. The school eventually got in touch with my mom, who agreed that she would enroll me in correspondence school if I had to be registered somewhere. Good. It fulfills legal requirements, and I don't have to explain why I'm not in class. I have too many other things to deal with. Other things included the fact that some of the new friends that were now suddenly around seemed to be bringing even more problems.

One specific problem was theft. We had two "break-ins" after we started dealing with a few specific people. They first took money and a TV. Then they came another time and took some of my mom's prescriptions and trashed the house. Luckily, they didn't stick around to visit after they did the second theft, but it was strange that my mom didn't seem to have a big problem with them. It was actually one of our other regular visitors that talked to my mom and told her she was getting too careless in who she was bringing into the house. Mom, of course, took the position that it was her home and she could invite anyone she wanted, thieves included. *What!? What kind of argument is that? Okay, fight for your right to get ripped off.*

I never knew what to say when my mom fought so hard for something so off base, so I just left the discussion and waited to see what would happen. Mom didn't apologize for her position of inviting anyone she wanted, but did eventually concede that the neighbor was trying to tell her something important. We went back to the usual social group and got back to what we always did – parties, dating, and drinking.

I would still go through efforts to look at my mom a lot to see if we could find our connection and rebuild our bond, but it seemed the disconnect between us had gotten worse. It felt much as I knew it to be in the past with my mom being really angry with me for a lot of the things that were going on. We were sometimes okay when we worked together, but then we would go into periods where she seemed to hate that I didn't want to fit into the lifestyle we lived.

She didn't get why I didn't like her boyfriends and rejected advances from different people but reminded me that I couldn't be too picky about who I would say yes to. She also really punished me for my decision not to become a drinker. She would tell me that if I didn't want to be a part of the group, then I would be treated as though I weren't. Then she would completely ignore me—actually acting as though I was not physically in the room. When friends came over, they were told to ignore me and were even told to leave if they didn't go along. I think it further disappointed my mom that this didn't work to encourage me to break down and join the group. Instead, I challenged her behavior as a mother and confronted her constant push to make me fit into a life I didn't want. Neither of us seemed to get what we wanted from each other, but still we moved on.

***

Don was one of Marcus's friends. I'm not sure exactly when he showed up, but he was suddenly there a lot. Mom dated him for a while but only with Marcus's approval. Mom liked Marcus and didn't want to drive him away, especially since he was bringing groceries and hadn't made advances toward her or me up to this point.

I was actually disappointed when Marcus finally made an attempt with me. He took the good guy approach and told me he wanted me to know what to expect when I found a guy. Just like his advice on how to make sure I'm not hit, he was offering to help me learn how not to get hurt during sex. I remember looking at him, watching him play this game, and wanting to ask him why he was doing it. I told myself to take a good look, because the friend I thought I had who was willing to talk to me about hard questions was not one I could trust. He was a game player, I had to know that. I didn't argue or confront his false friendship, but I did turn down his offer and tried to forget about it. I didn't talk about it, but the situation did come up when I was with someone else.

I tried to avoid being alone with Don, because he made my skin crawl. He seemed creepy and frightening. I can't say why. There was nothing specific that stood out about him—I just didn't trust anything about him. He came by one night when I was alone in the room. I told him that my mom was out, and I'd have her see him the next day. But he didn't take the hint and instead came in and made himself comfortable as he always did when my mom was there.

I got nervous very quickly. Don and I had no connection. We didn't chat. There was nothing we did together. There was, in fact, no reason for him to be there with me at all. I felt the same worry I had felt many times before and knew he would attempt to approach me.

In this situation, though, we were in the big room, so there was a lot of space to cover and two doors that could allow me to get out. He was on the chair near the far door at first. That was good. I wanted him to stay seated so it would give me just a few more seconds to get out if needed.

He started talking, mostly about things I didn't pay attention to, but then he eventually got to the topic of if I wanted to have sex. I said no and told him he should keep that between him and my mom or whoever he was dating. He said that he wasn't dating my mom anymore and then asked if we could just play around or even just kiss. I kept saying no and told him that I was tired and he should head out for the night.

He kept talking and eventually asked, "Would you say yes to Marcus?" I had a quick flash of memory when just a couple days earlier Marcus had approached me. I was suddenly mixed with the fear I had of Don and a deeper sense of betrayal from Marcus. I knew that night he was a false friend, but what exactly was up with this question from Don?

I asked him why he would say that, and he went on to tell me about the game he and Marcus were playing. It was a contest to see who I would say yes to. And if I wasn't going to say yes to Don, there was no way Marcus was going to win. Don got up from the chair when he said that to me, and I wasn't sure what he was going to do. *Is he going to force something here?*

I tried to keep calm and not show any fear while I walked over to the side door, which had the chain lock on it. I discreetly pressed the room buzzer four times then went on through the motions of getting something to drink and offered something to Don just to buy some time. He made me more nervous as he walked over to me. I headed toward the sink to get some glasses. He followed and tried to lean in to approach me, but I moved quickly to avoid him. And before he could move again, there was a knock at the door. I responded quickly and opened the door to see that it was David once again coming to my aid.

David had also found work at the hotel and was covering the front desk that night. Months ago we had made an agreement that if there were any problems, I could buzz four times and he would come up to help. This night he showed up with a stick in his hand and a pleasant offering in his voice saying he was just checking in to see how things are going. I opened the door completely to show him that I was not alone. I said things were fine and that I was going to go to bed soon, Don was just leaving. For everyone's sake, I am glad that the situation was resolved when Don saw I had help and decided to go. David waited to see Don leave and later came by to make sure he hadn't returned that night.

Back in Line

After the whole situation with Marcus and Don playing their little game, I thought there would be few things left that would surprise me. Then a day came that proved me wrong. I was pretty good at paying attention and anticipating things that would come up, but this day got me. After over a year of my leaving Luis and completely cut off communication with him and his family, Silvia showed up at the hotel to see my mom.

As soon as I walked into the room, I felt myself trying to hold in my panic. I knew nothing good could come from her being here. Silvia, I learned quickly, was there to talk to my mom about me. Luis, she said, had gotten worse. His anger was out of control, and he was always talking about how to kill himself. She said that I was a part of his life that gave him some sense of calm, so she had to try to get me to go back. These were things that had been said between them before I walked into the room and then explained to me as soon as I got there.

When I first walked in, my mom told me to sit down so we could talk. Her voice was the same as the one she used when Luis had talked to her after hitting me and telling her he really deeply loved me and just wanted to learn how to be a better man, because that's what I deserved. She sounded like she had found a wounded deer that she was determined to nurse back to health even if it was at my expense.

After she repeated the details of the conversation, I just froze and looked at my mom. I didn't want to believe what was happening. I had really worked to break away from someone who hit me. I know Mom didn't like it, but I did get away and needed to find a way to stay out of that life. Now she wants me to go back? Yes. I genuinely think she does.

I looked in her eyes hoping to connect, hoping she would recognize I'm her daughter and I was too young to be with a man I was supposed to take care of as my husband, even if I could figure out a way to keep from getting hit.

I remembered how it was true that when I was with Luis and went along as though this would be my whole life, Mom did like me more. *Maybe all the work I am doing to figure out how to find a different way to live is a waste of time. Am I ready to really be on my own knowing the options I have found so far? What if I say yes now but then later tell my mom I want to leave? I don't think that is part of the deal.*

So familiar, the feeling of having to make such absolute decisions. I go from being completely discouraged in life overall to feeling overwhelming fear and then anger. Then it's back to fear and a loss of hope. I remember so many immediate decisions I've had to make. *Speak up and hurt everyone or be strong enough to take it? Call the police to keep Mom from killing someone even if it humiliates her in public? Beg not to be hit, or just work with the rules of making sure the bruises aren't seen?* Again, the voices of so many people come back to me, telling me that this is the easy part and that the real problems start when you're an adult. I'm really not going to make it. Maybe it's time to stop looking around and just do what I am told. I doubt I can really do that, but the truth is no, I'm not ready to lose Mom.

I'm sure it was just a moment, but it felt like an hour had passed with me just sitting there, looking for my mom to see me and recognize what she was asking me to do. Nothing came back from her other than this almost excited look telling me she could be happy again if I said yes . . . then we'd go back to how things were for a little while when she liked me.

I felt completely betrayed and so full of anger at that moment. I couldn't believe that I was sitting between these two fully grown women who were there to talk about how to do what's right and keep this guy from killing himself and that somehow the answer was for me to agree to give my life away. *Is this how it happens?* Am I supposed to believe that women are just supposed to agree and walk open-eyed into lives of being targets as long as it's good for their men? Or to be more accurate, are girls supposed to be convinced by women that this is the best kind of life to grow into? No one said that Luis was going to take care of me or learn to stop hitting. The only talk was of how valuable I was in keeping him calm and giving him a reason to live. I was told that it was my decision, but it should be clear that he needs me and I could do something about his pain.

In hearing them try to convince me to "make my own decision" to go back to him, I wasn't convinced that he so desperately needed me or that it was my job to save him, but it became clear that the only real decision here was if I was going to have a place in the family. My mother would not say that I wouldn't, but she had already shown that she could make the decision to erase me and that she enjoyed my being with Luis as long as there were no facial bruises.

I knew I didn't want to go back, but I also knew I couldn't say no to my mom. In a real way, I still hate myself for this moment . . . but once again, my heart sank as I made the decision to just bow my head and agree to go along. I felt my hope for any vision of a future die when I said yes to returning to Luis's side. The relief I saw in Silvia and the happiness I saw in my mom that came from my decision did not give me any sense of comfort but instead reinforced what I already knew: I had no room to create my own life but instead had to accept that it was time to just take my place and go back, the same way Mom had in Barstow.

Epilogue

Another night of negotiating.
I know he has his pressures and he is trying to
figure out his life.

But, I need to sleep and not get hit. I won't fight
for my peace or my room tonight;
I need to stop fighting altogether.

I will apologize and tell him to sleep
on the bed. I will stay up.

Once he lays down, I can rest on the couch.
I will make sure the bedroom door is closed
so I hear if he opens it and I can
run out the front door if I have to.

I will know by the sound.
If he opens it softly, I can stay.
I am fading; I close my eyes to sleep.

I am on an empty road, or more like a trail
somewhere far away from a city. Emptiness
again, by myself, this is too familiar.
I am tired. I see a tree up the hill, it is nearly
bare, looking almost dead.

I gasp when I feel the pressure on my stomach
and all the wind is pushed out of my lungs.

Something has wrapped itself around me,
lifted me quickly and took me up, above the tree.

I was terrified at first, then almost immediately
comforted. The energy that has lifted me is there
to assure me.

It tells me to look closer – the tree is not dead.
It's still alive. I just need to get to it.

It feels like an overwhelming trek, but even if I
think I am alone, the world around me is still
here… more than what I live with, more than
what hurts me, more than I could imagine.

Just get to the tree; I will wrap you again if it's
needed. Now, wake up and make your way.

I am awake. I opened my eyes and felt myself
being held – wrapped and protected by whatever
was with me. I looked at the couch beneath me,
I was in the same apartment that I fell asleep in.

I am awake. How do I get back?
I was given no answer, but closed my eyes and
then told myself to look again.

I was back on the couch. There was no noise or worry about that night.

I knew that my job was to look for life –
somewhere outside of the world I lived in.
It will take a long time, but I can
ask to be lifted if needed.

Now, where do I start?

Staying In It

After the day of Silvia's visit, I got a call from Luis and soon after I went to see him. I resumed the relationship with a mentality that I had to figure out how to make things work. I was thirteen and had been successful in finding some kind of work most days of the week. But I was not strong enough to keep saying no to what was clearly being shown as what my life was supposed to be. I wasn't ready to move in with Luis and the Cruz family full time so I stayed with my mom at the hotel a couple more years. Luis would go back and forth between their place and the hotel before we moved back to Court Street, above the corner store and directly across from him and his family.

We were in that apartment when I was finally able to officially drop out of school. The correspondence course didn't last long and I had to enroll into seventh grade when we moved. Like the other years, I showed up enough to have some record, but missed weeks at a time. I didn't bother showing up when I was close to my 16th birthday and eventually told the social worker there was no need to call anymore.

The next few years were full of the same cycles but now I had lost almost all hope that things could be different. I did keep fighting and looking for something else just in my efforts to stay sober in an alcoholic environment and insisting on family therapy. Roman, Mom, and I went to a few sessions with Ken, who was the therapist we saw. The group sessions didn't last long but I did get a few individual appointments. Ken was the first person who heard my experiences and pointed out that there was abuse in the environment. He was also the first person who told me that I was not able to *fix* my family. He told me that even if I used every minute of my time and every ounce of my strength, it simply was not in one person's ability to fix a family's problem. It took some time but I did eventually understand what he meant. I still, however, was not able to fully put aside the idea that my efforts to find something better shouldn't include bringing my family with me.

Once I turned 18, I saw myself in the same situation. Though the occurrence of physical abuse had greatly reduced, I was still in this space surrounded by alcoholism, emotional manipulation, and hopelessness. I started thinking more and more of suicide as a possibility. I worked out my plan and figured out my timing but kept looking to see if there was another way. The only thing that came up was leaving my family—a thought almost impossible to consider. I went through months of considering death and telling myself that when it got to be too much, that would be the day to take action.

Each day that went by I told myself that it was not yet unbearable, just make it one more day. I finally got to the day when I couldn't pull myself up. I was almost physically incapable of bringing myself to get out of bed. I told myself that it was time to accept that something had to change so I would either find a way out of living here with my mom and Luis, or I would concede that I was stuck and would move toward the exit plan.

I didn't want to take extreme measures so I started a mental dialog to get myself to move forward. I told myself that no one really paid attention anyway so all I had to do was go through the motions of the day so no questions are asked, but then look outside for something else. If I were going to have a chance at a different life, I would have to look outside of the one I had. I would have to figure out how to make enough money to pay rent and bills, not just a low cash under the table. I kept looking and soon found a job training program. I needed a high school diploma to get training so I took some time and got my GED. The training was a three-month data entry course which lead to my first legal job at the same school.

Once I was working full time, I was ready to leave my mother's home. At this point, she was starting to get sick. She had never been in good health in my lifetime and so many years of smoking and drinking were taking an obvious toll. Roman had been out of the house for a little while but with my moving out, he moved back in with Mom for a while.

My first apartment was just a few block from Court Street but I was not successful in moving by myself; Luis had come along. I said I wanted to have my own place and pointed out that I was the only one working but my attempts at individuality was no match to my fear of Luis or my mother's pressure.

The time Luis and I lived together away from my mom is hard to describe. In some ways it was the same as before. I took care of the bills and groceries and was constantly trying to look for things to get better. Luis and I had a lot of arguments where I started confronting him with his hitting much in the way I confronted my mom in Oklahoma. I told him he was making excuses in his angry outbursts and that he knew exactly what he was doing. After some hard arguments, he would eventually say that he would try to stop but he would need some other things sexually.

That part still confused me. I saw many times that it seemed something gets mixed up and sex became about violence. It was so familiar to me that I told myself that I was the one mistaken here and agreed to do things he wanted. The one condition I asked was that he stays mentally present. If he couldn't see or connect with me, then the sex would be over. That's where things kept going wrong and I just couldn't believe that what we had was anywhere near what a healthy sex life was supposed to be.

Luis acted very jealous, but not in a way that made me feel valued or protected. He would see someone look at me or I casually say hello to someone walking down the street and he would go over the top in his reaction, yelling, threatening, sometimes following people to start a fight. It felt the same way it did with the sex. I know he was going through the motions but I wasn't sure that he was actually fighting for me, or even considered me. I would hear women talk about how good it felt to be protected, but my thought was that what he was doing had nothing to do with me so I actually felt more threatened by his "protective" actions.

Still, we kept going along. I tried to own my role as being a good partner who would do what it takes to make things work, never because it was the life I wanted but because I had no vision for anything else. I wasn't able to keep the apartment for long. After just a couple years with my inability to break away from Luis and his constant presence with no financial contribution resulted in my giving up the apartment. I felt lost, like I was just floating. We ended up staying with Luis's family a little while. Then Mom got to a point where she was very sick and the tension between her and Roman was out of control. Roman and I talked and agreed that I would move back and take care of Mom and he would move out.

To no surprise, Luis had quickly all but completely moved in with me and Mom. It wasn't the life I wanted but at least my mom liked having me around now. We would sometimes try to enjoy life but more often than not, there was so much darkness it was hard to keep going. By the time I was in my twenty's the hitting had nearly completely stopped and the abuse had moved to mostly emotional manipulation. I was never strong enough to brush off emotional games that so many people seemed to be good at playing, but I found it impossible when my mother seemed to want me to go along which I did for nearly ten more years.

Getting Out

It wasn't until Mom died that I was able to get out of the life of abuse. It wasn't easy but I had been working for years to build up my strength and vision of possibilities. I spent much of my childhood trying to imagine a better life and in my twenties I spent a lot of time and energy on personal therapy.

I went to a couple of therapists that I quickly knew were not a good fit before I met one who was. When I first started with Iris, I still couldn't envision exactly what kind of life I was looking for, but I knew I had lost some part of myself that I needed to get back. I started working with Iris a few years before my mom died. I would go for a while and then take a break to try to practice some of the things we had talked about. Some of the basics like believing I had a right to change my mind about my decisions and create a different life was one of the first things to address.

As our sessions kept going, I was learning that much of what I needed was to *undo* some of the lessons I had been practicing, including that of denying anger. In that part of the work, we revisited the topic of my seizures several times and I eventually was able to understand that although I was diagnosed, my seizures were likely due to extreme experiences rather than epilepsy. No, I have not been medically examined for epilepsy since childhood, but with the work I have done personally, I believe epilepsy was a misdiagnoses.

Mom died of lung failure during the 1999 holiday season, after a long battle with multiple physical ailments. When she died, I was almost desperate to leave the house and rid my life of everything. I was lucky to have a good job and some friends who tried to support me. So I told myself that I not leave my job but would leave everything else. It took me three months to clean up all the trash in the house and find an apartment. I tried to stand my ground but still did not have the strength to get away from Luis. He followed me to the new apartment arguing that he had been practically living with us for so long it was only right that I plan for him too. I was able to take enough of a stand to say that he could come by but could not move in. It would have to be my home, not his. It should be no surprise that things did not go well. But I did eventually, after several months, succeed in telling Luis that he could not come back.

In transitioning to my own life away from Mom and away from Luis, I continued working with Iris. She pointed out that so much of the work I had been doing was in an attempt to leave my mother and now that she is gone, my work would be to allow for my own life. Though she was right, it took me years of efforts after separating myself from abusive personalities to start creating a life that was more than just about surviving. I went through long periods of deep depression and years of dealing with panic attacks where I was so afraid of walking down the street that I would often not be able to go more than a few steps away from home unless it was to go to work. I was glad to have a job just to give myself a reason to get up, though things did eventually get to be so overwhelming that I had to take a leave of absence.

I've done a lot of work to get to a point where I can be in my own skin without being in constant fear. I worry sometimes that in my current life of loving people and comfort, I will lose my strength and won't be able to figure out how to manage things if I do fall back into a life of abuse. I tell myself that part of life is over, but I still look for proof that it is true. I also still struggle with old fears that come up in sometimes crippling ways.

The truth is that I am not completely confident about having a life forever free of abuse, but at least I believe I now know the difference. I know that there is conflict in life that is healthy and have learned to have a real respect for the role and value of anger. I don't feel confused about the difference between a difficult relationship and an abusive one.

Though in moving toward a new life, I've had to develop a different kind of tolerance just to manage what most people consider normal activity and social events. Many of my experiences have been extreme with intense highs and lows coming so regularly that the things others see as normal often feel empty or untrue to me. I don't always know how to handle the empty space of waiting for the next event while distracting myself with things that seem so light in comparison to past situations.

It took me over a decade of adulthood and the death of my mother to leave an abusive life and has taken me another 15+ years to work through the emotional damage that came from so many harmful experiences. Yet I still struggle and am still so full of rage that I do not fully trust my own sense of safety. Clearly, I still have work to do.

About Mom,
About Forgiveness

Standing alone again at the same corner,
the 92 still stops here.
Everything is so empty;
I don't know where I'm going.

Was any of this worth it?
She's gone, but really,
nothing has changed; I can't stop crying, sobbing.

The sky is clear, the air is cool.
I hear her speaking
trying to comfort me

Her voice is gentle but still seems to fill the sky.
I listen with some comfort
when I recognize how clear her voice is, with all
disease gone.

"Things are okay; I'm okay.
No more pain. Things are clear now"
I have no voice but keep crying, wanting
her to know I am still lost.

I almost feel her touch in the air
stroking my eyebrows,
as she did when I was a girl.

"I'm sorry I didn't know how to take care of you.
I understand more now.
I can't explain but can only tell that everything
is the way it should be"
I want to ask how I could know
that truth but my voice is empty.

"There's so much more than I can say
I promise, honey, things really are
just right – you are just right."
Her words were attempts to reassure but still,
my only sounds were of crying.

"Don't try to think about it now.
You will know more. I promise."
I hear a melody; an old familiar song.

"You like this song, remember?
Sing it with me..."
I listen and try to sing but fail.

All I can find is a whispered hum from
deep in my chest.
"Yes, honey, keep going... sing with me...
I promise, everything is right...
it will all make sense"

Mom

More than 15 years after her death, I still miss my mom. I miss her moments of clarity when she showed me the most complete way to be with someone always involved compassion and an ability to listen. I miss her singing old songs and playing cards. I miss just being able to talk to her.

People often ask me how I feel about her considering everything that happened. Reactions to our relationship and how I handled things span from complete horror of how I could talk to my mom the way I did to total wonder of why I held, and still hold, the gifts my mother gave me so tightly. I guess I understand the judgments, good and bad, on some level. But none of them really refer to the whole picture. The idea that I should never confront my mom because of her role of a parent makes an assumption she is actually fulfilling that role. But in reality, in many ways, for many years, my mother simply didn't parent me in a safe and loving way. I fought my mom hard because I had to for my own clarity. The fact that I fought does not mean I did not see my mother's loving side.

As I work through my own efforts to learn and heal, I still look to my mom for comfort. I mean, the part of her that was clear, when she was in her best self. That is the part that I look to and imagine is here still with me. I recall and document frightening things that I remember and I imagine Mom not being ashamed of events but aware of the effects, knowing I am still here having to deal with them. When I was with my mom at her best, I never had to apologize for any part of myself and I stick with that position today. When I look at this work, I imagine Mom being here knowing that this is my voice and she expects no apology for it.

Forgiveness

Forgive and forget, or let go and let God.

So many people have told me that forgiving and letting go are the ways to find my own peace. I know that many others do find comfort in these approaches, but when I honestly answer the question if I forgive my mother, the answer is simply no.

This answer, not surprisingly, does offend some people as openly saying you do not forgive a parent seems harder for people to take than it is to know that a parent's repeated actions result in lifelong challenges that are not easy and sometimes impossible to overcome.

Admittedly, I don't remember (or more honestly, I have chosen to discard) much of what I was taught through Catholicism. I do recall, however, learning that the act of forgiveness is not a single action, but requires the offender to first acknowledge the offense, attempt to make amends, and ask for forgiveness. With this understanding, forgiveness is not applicable as these events did not occur. For me, acknowledgement is more appropriate than forgiveness.

I love my mom and will always credit her for giving me some of the lessons that continue to serve me in my life now. I don't know all the pain she endured in her life or the extent of how it affected her, but I do know that she had many difficulties throughout both her childhood and adulthood. I know that my mom was aware enough to recognize some things about what she believed hurt her. Specifically, she would talk about three things that were repeatedly discouraged through physical punishment or personal shaming: touching, physical mistakes like dropping things or falling, and asking questions.

With her awareness of these things, she made a very real effort not to punish me in the same way she was punished. Mom touched me every day: hugging, kissing, hand holding, rubbing on lotion, brushing hair, lots of physical connection that felt good. When I dropped things or fell, she never scolded or embarrassed me, but instead would just say that everyone falls or sometimes things break. As for asking questions, this is possibly the most important thing my mother gave me – repeated permission to ask any question that came up. Even if she didn't know the answer and even if she didn't want to talk about the issue. She might not answer, but I was never told to stop questioning. And, asking my questions, consistently, repeatedly, and directly, is something I genuinely believe has helped me overcome many obstacles simply because posing a question allows a suggestion that there may be a different option than what is immediately in front of me. For this specifically, I will always credit my mom for helping me.

Honestly, I could list many lessons my mother gave me. I can also see the vision of her as a person who went through years of her own abuse and did not have a parent to tell her it was okay if she made a mistake. I have really looked to see my mom as more than the person who raised me, but someone who never did figure out some of the important things, and still somehow was so clear about other things. I know she was a whole person deserving of love and compassion, both of which I will always have for her. Forgiveness is a completely different concept that doesn't belong in the description of what I feel for or think of my mother.

Gratitude

I want to acknowledge those in my life who have contributed to my growth and success in completing this very personal project. I am fortunate to be surrounded by people who freely offer love and support.

Thank you all, for listening, talking, staying up with me, holding my hand, reminding me of successes, sharing your perspectives, and believing in this effort.

I also want to share a note of gratitude to Iris Nathaniel for years of help in personal therapy. I still look to lessons from our work together as I continue moving forward.

No words can express the depth of my gratitude for the love, support, and encouragement I have enjoyed from so many wonderful people in my life. Thank you.

Made in the USA
Middletown, DE
19 October 2017